Arquine

works.voices

25

25 Works, 25 Voices

First edition, 2022

Ámsterdam 163 A, Hipódromo
Mexico City, 06100
ISBN: 978-607-9489-97-7

Directors and Editors
Miquel Adrià, Andrea Griborio

Publishing Director
Brenda Soto

Publishing Coordinator
Ana Luz Valencia

Design
Cristina Paoli · Periferia

Copy Editing
Gwennhael Huesca

Translation
Gregory Dechant

www.arquine.com

Miquel Adrià
Andrea Griborio

works.voices 25

25 benchmark **works** built in **Latin America** in the last **25 years** that have resisted the onslaught of time with dignity

25 Works & 25 Voices

Arquine, a platform that has kept abreast of global architecture from the vantage point of Mexico for the last quarter century, gathers in this volume twenty-five extraordinary works constructed in Latin America over the last twenty-five years, reference points in the development of the discipline that have withstood the buffeting of time. Twenty-five architects have been invited each to choose a project and write about it. This compendium seeks to lend added value to the history of the architecture produced so far in the twentieth century and, if possible, to mark a before and after, in global terms, about what it means to practice architecture under the conditions of each place.

To establish the context, we need to recall that 1997 was the year that cellphones stopped having external antennas. Bill Clinton began his second term that year and Tony Blair was elected prime minister of Great Britain. It was in 1997 that Lady Di and Gianni Versace died, as well as Allen Ginsberg and William Burroughs, Jacques Cousteau and Mother Teresa, Félix Candela and Aldo Rossi. It was the year that César Pelli's Petronas Towers were built —the highest buildings in the world until 2003—, along with Renzo Piano's Beyeler Foundation Museum and the Kunsthaus Bregenz of Peter Zumthor. Above all, it was the year of Frank Gehry's Guggenheim Museum in Bilbao.

Mexico in 1997 was still suffering the hangover induced by the euphoria of the Salinas years and the collapse of the peso in late 1994: the country was in the throes of the recovery efforts of the administration of Ernest Zedillo. It was toward the end of 1997 that the first issue of *Arquine* appeared, a publishing project in the form of a quarterly magazine/journal which has grown since then to include competitions, congresses, the publication of books, radio and television shows, academic programs, and exhibitions. It has enriched and helped to reorient architectural culture in Mexico, Latin America, and around the world.

Arquine has published material about almost all of the works included in this book, which when they appeared were generally *news*, owing either to the quality of the designs or to the timeliness of their construction. Some of the projects were immediately reviewed or commented on in the print version of *Arquine* or on its website (www.arquine.com). Monographs were published about others —the school of architecture of the Universidad de Talca, the Biblioteca Vasconcelos, La Tallera, the Museo Jumex, the Archivo General del Estado de Oaxaca, the Centro Cultural Teopanzolco— or they were the subject of indivudual chapters in books covering the entire careers of the architects.

It is true that most of the architects gathered together here will come as no surprise. They are established professionals whose careers we have all been able to follow: from unquestioned masters (such as Rogelio Salmona and Teodoro González de León—whose shared origins go back to Le Corbusier's studio at 35, rue de Sèvres—, Álvaro Siza, Paulo Mendes da Rocha, and David Chipperfield) to architects who have become references in the best of Latin American architecture (the Colombians Felipe Uribe, Daniel Bonilla, and Camilo Restrepo; the Chileans Alejandro Aravena/

ELEMENTAL, Teresa Moller, Germán del Sol, Smiljan Radic, Paula Velasco, and Cecilia Puga; the Peruvians Sandra Barclay and Jean Pierre Crousse; the Paraguayan Solano Benítez; and the Mexicans Isaac Broid, Alberto Kalach, and Mauricio Rocha), as well as others who have recently burst onto the global scene as revelations from the Americas (Al Borde, from Ecuador; HLPS, from Chile; and Frida Escobedo, Tatiana Bilbao, and PRODUCTORA, from Mexico). It should perhaps be specified (however obvious to any reader of *Arquine*) that the presence of a work in Latin America was sufficient to justify its inclusion, even if the architect was from a country outside the region. In addition to Siza and Chipperfield, mentioned above, we will also find here the Spanish architect Ignacio Mendaro Corsini, author of the Archivo General del Estado de Oaxaca.

If the works selected are all in some way watersheds in the history of Latin American architecture over the last quarter century, the twenty-five voices that describe, dissect, analyze, and comment on them are intentionally of the same stature. They are all peers: architects who dialogue with respect, critical acumen, and in some cases open admiration, and who present reflections that have been refined over the course of the years. The texts are not abstracts or descriptions of the projects, but brief essays, as fascinating as they are revealing about the before and after of the works themselves, about everything that has never been written down.

Inclusion in this book is not a prize, but it is a confirmation that the quality of the designs that we initially considered outstanding has continued to brave the passage of time. Early in this century, Oscar Tusquets established the Premio Década, which honors architectural works that are ten years old, with a view to "assessing how a building has aged, but also how relevant to the present a project conceived ten years ago continues to be."[1] With axiomatic concision, he lays out two criteria: that any construction can be architecture —interiors, buildings, restorations, or urban spaces— and that a work can only be assessed in its context. From a similar perspective, we have selected twenty-five projects that have stood up over the last twenty-five years and have aged well. Architecture is a long-term discipline and good constructions tend not only to last, but even to perpetuate themselves. There are no new works included here: all of them have ripened over the years and we now consider them the very best of the harvest.

During this period, many works have been speedily forgotten and their architects have disappeared like shooting stars. This is not the place to list these fiascos, since often it is the pressure from governments, eager to make a mark and inaugurate supposedly white elephants —though they come in all colors, depending on the government in turn—, that has done no more than trivialize architecture with triumphalist airs. The selection made here seeks to transcend these circumstances of haste and opportunism by presenting twenty-five works that *exist* in their own right. Some helped to spearhead processes of urban transformation, such as the Parque de los Pies Descalzos, by +UdeB Arquitectos, in Medellín, Colombia, or Quinta Monroy, by ELEMENTAL, in Iquique, Chile, which has become a replicable model. Others belong to sustained series of projects that are best understood as "choral" works, such as the interventions into the landscape of the Central Valley in Chile by the school of architecture of the Universidad de Talca. Some works considered lesser, or perhaps even marginal, when we originally published them have ripened with time and use, owing to their inherently timeless qualities or to the correctness

1 "The Four Commandments of the Década Prizes," Oscar Tusquets Blanca: http://www.tucquotc.oom/fundaoion otb/promioo dooada/10 anoo dc arquitcotura-en-barcelona.

of design decisions, such as chapel of the Colegio Los Nogales by Daniel Bonilla in Bogotá, Colombia, or the educational farm pavilions of Mónica Bertolino and Carlos Barrado in Argentina.

Still others have been considered masterpieces ever since they were constructed and continue to constitute the most outstanding works in their respective countries. Such is the case of the Orquideorama by AGENdA, JPR Arquitectos and Plan:B, in Medellín, which originally astonished by its originality and then flourished as part of successive urban transformation programs, remaining an icon of that prolific period that put the City of Eternal Spring on the global map. No less important is the Biblioteca Vasconcelos in Mexico City, a project led by Alberto Kalach following an unusual international competition. This piece of urban equipment has surprised us all by its timeless and archaic monumentality. In spite of the neglect it has suffered from a series of fratricidal federal administrations, it has survived like a great vessel beached after a storm.

Years later, three works fundamental to Latin America were built: the Place of Memory, Tolerance, and Social Inclusion designed by Sandra Barclay and Jean Pierre Crousse in Lima; the Centro Cultural Teopanzolco, by Isaac Broid in collaboration with PRODUCTORA, in Cuernavaca; and the Teatro Regional del Biobío, by Smiljan Radic, in Concepción, Chile. We can add the offices of the Fundacão Iberê Camargo, by Álvaro Siza, in Porto Alegre; the Biblioteca Pública Virgilio Barco, by Rogelio Salmona, in Bogotá; and the Museo Universitario Arte Contemporáneo, by Teodoro González de León, in Mexico City, all projects of impeccable quality by great contemporary masters working around the close of their careers.

We especially admire those works that intervene in the landscape, such as the hot spring complex designed by Germán del Sol in Coñaripe and the stone path, all but sculpted, by Teresa Moller at the Punta Pite residential development in Zapallar (both in Chile), as well as the botanical garden in Culiacán, Mexico, by Tatiana Bilbao. We might also include in this category the project of Las Tres Esperanzas by the Ecuadoran team Al Borde, where understanding the landscape has consisted of obtaining materials to provide better living conditions to a community whose only resources were enthusiasm and ingenuity.

Also fundamental are those interventions that involve the recycling of a preexisting construction, such as La Tallera, executed by Frida Escobedo in Cuernavaca; the Centro Cultural San Pablo, by Mauricio Rocha and Gabriela Carrillo, in Oaxaca; the SESC 24 de Maio, designed by Paulo Mendes da Rocha in collaboration with MMBB in São Paulo; the Parque Cultural de Valparaíso, by HLPS; and the newly equipped Palacio Pereira, by Cecilia Puga, Paula Velasco, and Alberto Moletto, in Santiago de Chile, which, in spite of being the most recent work of the selection, with a restoration process that has lasted more than ten years, is already considered a notable new heritage site in the country.

Although we began with a short list of forty works, the authors of the twenty-five essays determined by their own choices the contents of the book. In this way, we avoided a selection based on proportional representation in terms of the countries or generations to which the architects belonged. We were also interested in weaving a narrative by means of the order of the texts, which is chronological (based on date of construction), rather than alphabetic or determined by location. An accurate reading of the architecture of Latin America necessarily reflects the social and political processes that accompanied it.

It is not entirely by chance that the book begins and ends with works in Chile, for good design has tended to be a constant in that country. This can perhaps be interpreted as a product of its stability and growth over the last two decades, during which time architecture as cultural policy has enjoyed strong public support. The Colombian projects have grouped themselves —with no help from us— into the period of the late 1990s and early 2000s, when the need to transform many of the cities in the country was high on the public agenda. The Mexican projects begin to appear in 2007, as the political transition generated a certain increase in public infrastructure construction. Brazil remains a unique case, as ever, while the rest of the works appear as orbiting satellites that interconnect realities and hopes in a region endeavoring to build common signs of identity and to intertwine the cultures of unconnected places.
May this selection serve as a sampling of the best architecture carried out in Latin America over the last twenty-five years, to be compared not only with that of the United States, Europe, and Japan, but also with that of other regions on the planet, ever more thriving and doubtless of great interest as well. During a period of economic crisis, which left global architectural production tottering, even as it undermined the hegemony of the United States and certain European countries, Latin American and Chinese works, along with those of other Asian countries, emerged as innovative proposals that have attracted the attention of critics, academia, and the media. Tools like this book help to lend a certain uniformity to information about the region's most outstanding architectural production, in addition to sharing the best of Latin America with a wider public.

School of Architecture of the Universidad de Talca

In the atmosphere of Talca there is always a hint of poetry. In order to understand what we are referring to when we talk about the school of architecture of the Universidad de Talca, we have to strip ourselves of our prejudices about what architecture, school, and space all signify, and to think of the elements that configure a place: its cultural landscape, the processes of working it, and matter as a tool for teaching. "The Talca way involves taking a lot of risks," as Juan Román, the creator of the school, pointed out, when I asked him if it was possible to replicate this educational model in other parts of Latin America. We are dealing with a place that "sounds like one thing and turns out to be so many."[1]

The school is halfway between Santiago de Chile and Concepción. One of the most authentic manifestations of Chilean culture has emerged in this agricultural zone of the Central Valley. In 1998, the Universidad de Talca decided to establish a school of architecture and charged Juan Román —an architect graduated in 1983 from the Universidad de Valparaíso— with drawing up a plan of studies and acting as the new school's first director. Thus began an educational project, recognized for its innovate approach, which has

1 Andrea Griborio, "Cuando el paradigma es la educación. Breve entrevista a Juan Román," *Zona de Proyecto* no. 19.

managed to evolve and transform itself by attending to the values and historical baggage of the students it accepts. Many of these young people are the first in their families to receive a higher education. All of them are eager to learn and they bring skills —though not necessarily academic knowledge— from the places where they were raised, each with its particular matter and culture.

"Talca, Paris, and London" is a phrase belonging to the oral tradition of this unexceptional place in the Central Valley, a phrase which fills *talquinos* with pride, because it evokes a glorious past, when Talca was the third most populous town in Chile.[2] Battles against forgetfulness are waged daily in this territory: a forgetfulness that translates into neglect by the "center" of the country and its policies conceived in the big cities, indifferent to the problems of the periphery and to non-urbanized zones. And also the neglect of academic institutions, in which teaching is standardized without regard for a basic question asked frequently in Talca, which is the key to its unique model: where do I teach architecture?[3]

2 "Talca, París y Londres: origen del dicho." See the website of the Museo O'Higginiano y de Bellas Artes de Talca: https://www.museodetalca.gob.cl/colecciones/talca-paris-y-londres-origen-del-dicho.

3 Juan Ignacio Baixas, Alberto Sato, Juan Román, and Albert Tidy, "Cuatro escuelas de arquitectura," *ARQ* 61 (2005), pp. 17-24.

The first visible signs of the school of architecture appeared in 2004, with the construction of the first "signed" pieces, but the idea that the students would begin to construct from the time they were still taking course had been conceived in the year 2000. Understanding the student as a "builder" transcended the traditional idea of learning-by-doing, which in architecture schools often ends up as learning-by-representing. In Talca, the training of an architect was conceived in a manner more appropriate to the apprentice architect's context and knowledge. According to Juan Román, this method of training of architects with coherence, optimism, and honesty (and a little bit of luck), has awakened the interest of many people, thanks to the work of the school in Talca. And it has taken Talca to places never imagined before.

The Talca way seeks to produce qualified professionals. Professionals capable of building a common sense. It is not simply a question of seeing what they know in another way, but rather of bringing out the potential of the community they carry within themselves, in order to give shape to the idea of the collective from and within the territory. There is an important element of the "normal school" (a school that trains teachers) in Talca. This little percentage of variation, as in a DNA sequence, is what makes this project one of the most significant works of architecture in Latin America over the last twenty-five years. This fragment creates an ability in the students to do and manage things, to deal with their own family baggage. The results have been both beautiful and meaningful.

The idea is to build something somewhere. In spaces like the matter workshop, which is given in the first year of the program, the students work with the stuff of their own experiences to generate playful and enriching results. In the project workshop, from the second to the fifth year, plazas and other collective spaces are designed. For their graduation theses, the students conceive, design, finance, organize, and build small works in which the skills they have acquired are tested. Therein resides the singularity of this educational project, consisting of small works, in which the figure of the signature architect disappears to make way for the construction of a new landscape, one that respects and enriches the rural and agricultural territory and customs of places like the Central Valley and provides material to improve the way people actually live.

As a privileged witness to this process of transformation over time, this volume opens with the School of Architecture of the Universidad de Talca, in which the idea of "signature architecture" is dissolved to make way for architectures originating on the periphery, with attention to ways of inhabiting and the people who inhabit them. This selection of twenty-five emblematic works from all over Latin America may be complemented, less substantially, by some of the proposals constructed "against the tide," which have left small traces on the Chilean landscape, a rural landscape, like so much of Latin America.[4] The project began around the start of the period covered by this book and shares a map to locate this constellation of landmarks and to display some of the works that have contributed to raising the profile of the school. Talca produces and manages processes and objects that originate in an understanding of and dialogue with the landscape. It continues today to insert devices conceived according to this singular academic model, devices which serve communities, weave narratives, and occupy the landscape of the Central Valley in the way that territory has been built: with what there is at hand.

Andrea Griborio

4 "A contracorriente" [Against the Tide], by Juan Román and José Luis Uribe, was the Chilean pavilion at the 15th International Architecture Exhibition of the Venice Biennale.

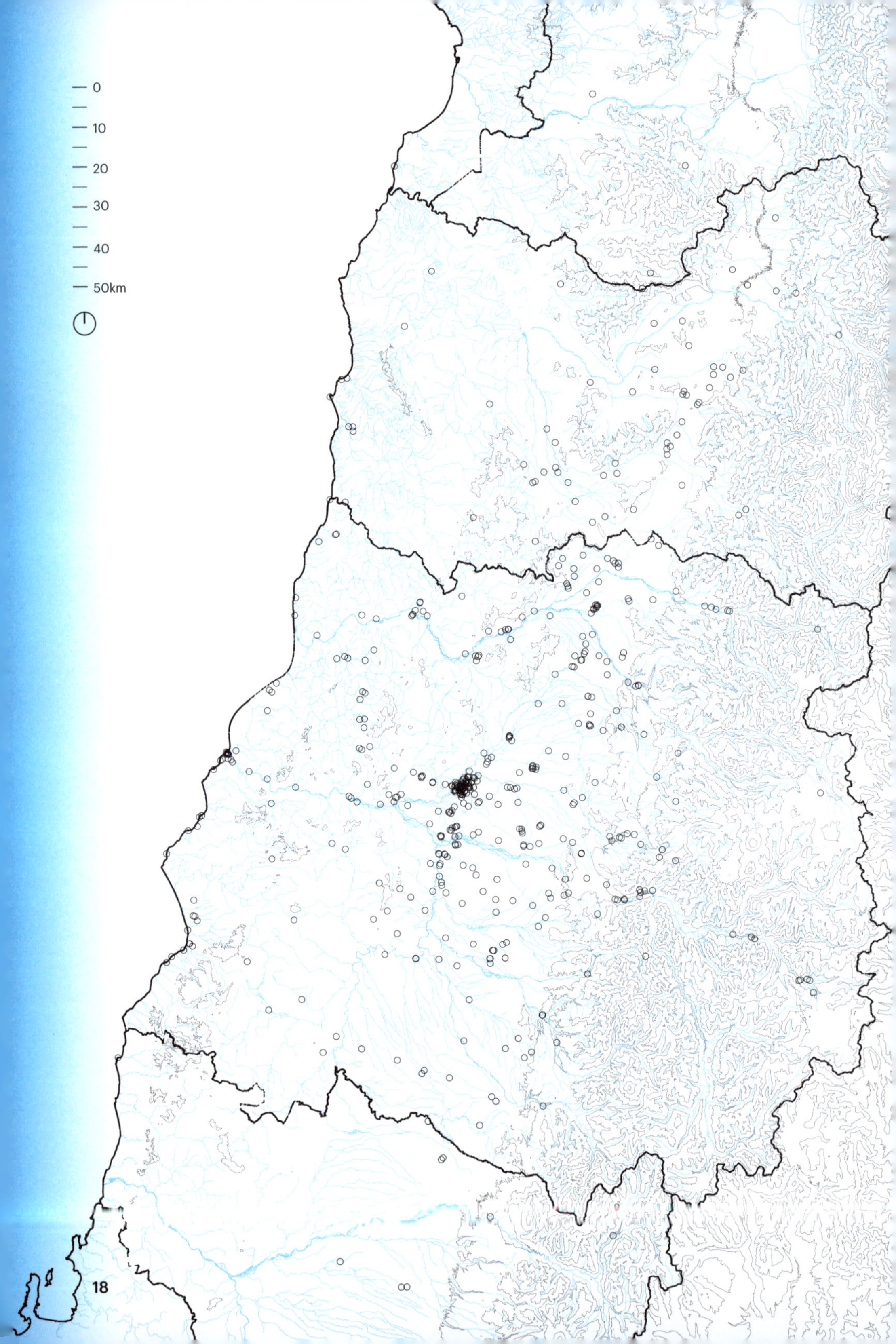
0
10
20
30
40
50km

2006. Storage facility and viewpoint in Pinohuacho. Rodrigo Sheward.

2007. Landmark: inner rainfed route. Ronald Hernández, Marcelo Valdés, Osvaldo Veliz.

2007. Chilean-style race pavilion. Claudio Castillo.

2008. Pleamar shelter. Daniel Prieto.

2009. Collection and dining hall for raspberry orchards. Ximena Céspedes.

2011. Special activities classroom. Luis Calquín.

2011. Outstanding lookout and eating area. Javier Rodríguez.

2011. Infiernillo station. Mauricio Ureta.

2011. Salíneas, a place for history. Felipe Aranda.

2012. Remains facing the horizon. Felipe Muñoz.

2012. Agua Santa ceremony plaza. Ximena Cáceres.

2013. Pallets plaza. Jonnattan Silva.

2014. Sunshade in a Chilean-style race court. Carolina Solís.

2015. Open corral refuge. Edgard Torres.

2016. In resistance to the local memory. Katherine Chávez Carrillo.

2017. Descending through the rocks. Angélica Méndez.

2018. Pehuenche commemorative landmark. Antonia Ossa.

2018. Conversion of San Pedro thermal baths. Pía Montero.

2019. Trafwe Ültu Pire / Shelter for tents in the snow. María Jesús Molina.

2022. Lookout tower Arbolillo. Hangysan Sanhueza.

Parque de los Pies Descalzos

The Moment of the Dark Street

At that time we were wondering what to do, questioning our own role as citizens. The 1990s were a critical period in Medellín, but also a time of collective interaction in the search for answers. The historian Jorge Orlando Melo has described it all in detail in his book *Los años difíciles* [The Difficult Years]. We used to refer to that period as "the dark street," when we had lost the city and it was impossible to come together in the streets, in public spaces. As a result, we locked ourselves in, and the city filled up with protected enclaves.

It was not a moment for architects to be playing a public role in Medellín. What came afterwards, when our role in the city was decisive in creating a new story, were the dreams of a large group of young architects just setting out on their careers. I remember when we were hungry for relevant referents and traveling companions. The school of architecture at the Universidad Pontificia Bolivariana (UPB) became a laboratory of ideas and collaborations. We had the privilege of welcoming as guests many of the architects and urban planners who were transforming Spain at the time. The *maestros* ('teachers,' but also 'masters') who had led the process of change in Barcelona were particularly generous with their time and friendship. Today I see it all clearly: it was a pivotal moment on the path that many of us would later take.

On this journey of discovery, Manuel de Solà-Morales and the Laboratori d'Urbanisme de Barcelona (LUB) —part of the Escola Tècnica Superior d'Arquitectura de Barcelona— played a special role. Solà-Morales's visit to Medellín in those years was decisive in the creation of the Laboratorio de Arquitectura y Urbanismo (LAUR) of the UPB a few years later. I can also affirm that the founding ideas of the LAUR were given concrete form in an initial project: the Parque de los Pies Descalzos ('Barefoot Park'). The friends who led that workshop translated with mastery many of the dreams we all shared at the time. We longed for good design, good urban architecture, to be the main agent of change, the path toward a fair, open city of collective encounters.

From 1998 to 2001 I was in Barcelona, studying Medellín. I had the good fortune to be welcomed by the faculty of the LUB. From a distance, I followed with great interest the whole process of the conception and development of the Parque de los Pies Descalzos, which for many of us was the watershed we were waiting for in order to champion a new urban design and open up an unlikely space in a confined and fearful city.

The park is in the center of the city, between the government buildings of La Alpujarra and the Medellín River. At the time this was a deteriorated urban polygon with absolutely no places for public encounters. Some important public infrastructure had been built, such as the Convention Center in 1975 and the Teatro Metropolitano in 1987, but these tended to operate from the doors inward, since the use of the street and of public space was virtually impossible, given the high levels of crime and violence. In 1996 the new head offices of the public utility group Empresas Públicas de Medellín (EPM) were inaugurated, and that is where the story of the park begins.

The context is made up of three large pieces of urban equipment, constructed in close proximity to each another over the course of twenty years, amidst parking areas and empty lots, with no possibilities of providing places of encounter for a city in crisis. The management of EPM wanted to spruce up the surroundings of their new head offices and turned to the newly-created LAUR for ideas. What began as a corporate complex produced, in the process, two unlikely and extraordinary external results: EPM realized the value of public space and began to assume a central role in the transformation of Medellín, while a relatively small and isolated site in a complicated zone was turned into a social success. For the first time in many years, the residents of Medellín were able to watch their children splashing in public wading pools and their friends and neighbors conversing (barefoot!) in central part of the city. We architects saw that urban design had been restored to us as a key tool in bringing people back outside.

I will not go into the processes or the urban and architectural components of the project, but there are three singular aspects that I would like to highlight: the construction of different scales in an isolated and fragmented environment; the skill with which different spaces were created as unique experiences; and the mastery of surface definition and design details in indicating the use of the different elements. The extraordinary thing about the Parque de los Pies Descalzos is how it has generated memories for so many users and offered them the possibility of experiencing private moments —meditating or exercising, enjoying time with the family or even falling in love—, while salvaging a place of collective encounter in a city where the streets were still dark.

Many things have happened in Medellín since the Parque de los Pies Descalzos was created: we have led a process of social urbanism for the neighborhoods of the city, the northern zone has advanced in its process of transformation, EPM has become a central agent and financial backer of emblematic projects —such as the articulated life units—, the Parques del Río footpath and cycling route has been constructed, and urban design is now an integral part of the story of the city. Nevertheless, this particular place marks an unforgettable moment in the history of Medellín. I carry an image in my mind of that moment when older adults found a place again in the city center, where they could rest their bare feet on the edge of a fountain and converse with friends.

Alejandro Echeverri

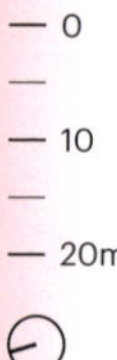

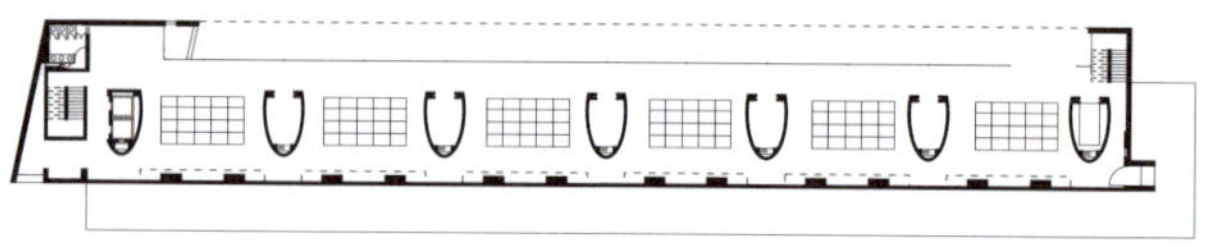

Level 2

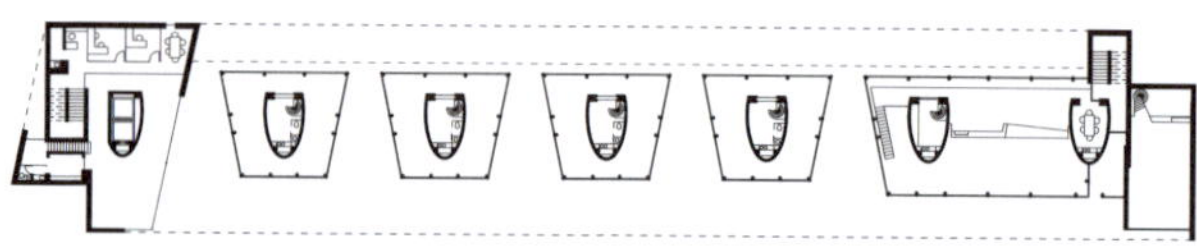

Mezzanine

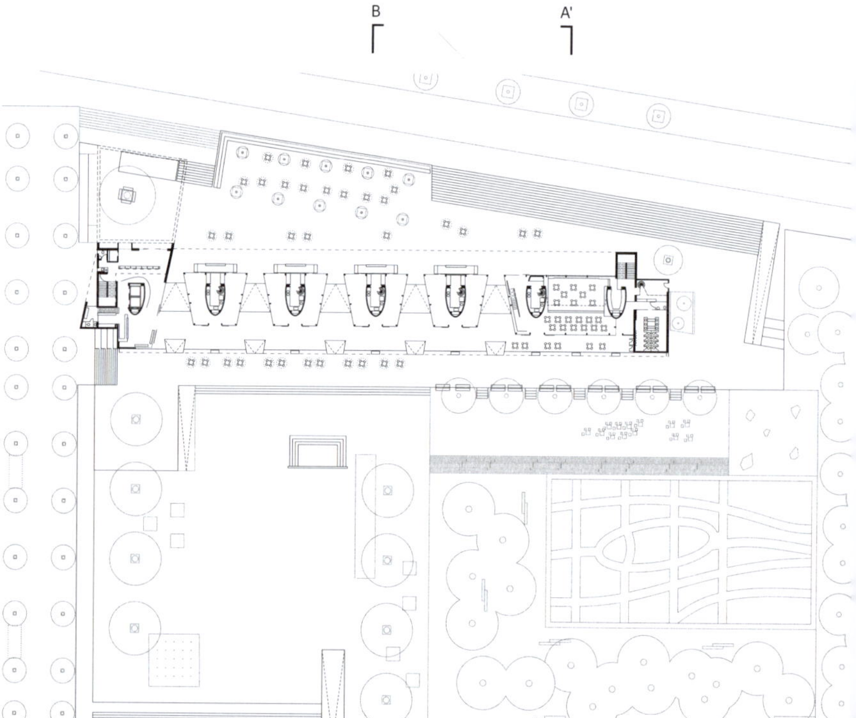

B A'

B' A

Ground floor plan

0
5
10m

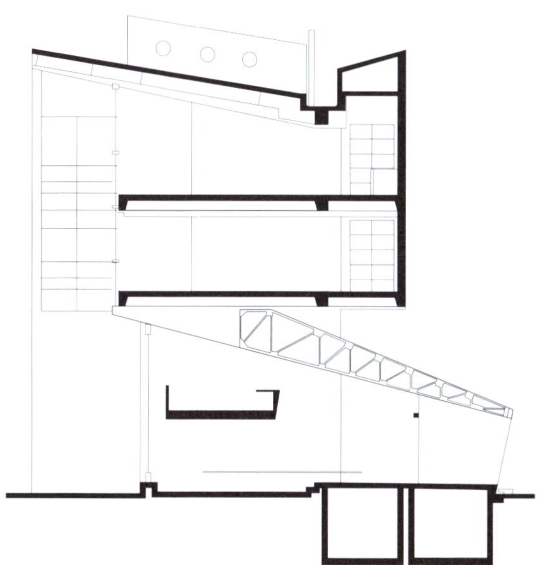

Section A-A'

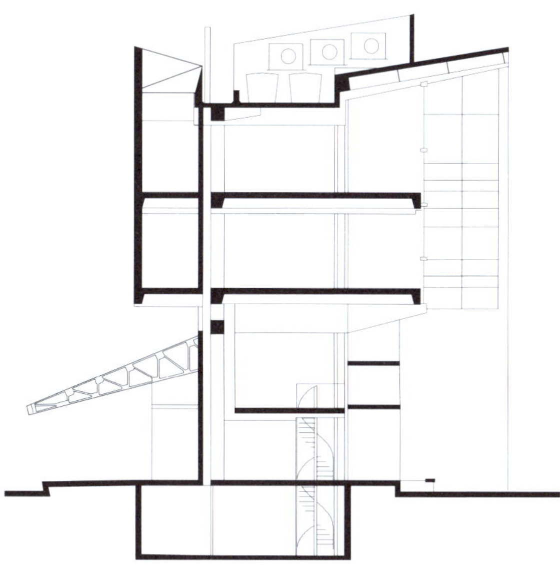

Section B-B'

Biblioteca Pública Virgilio Barco

A Cathedral of Books

When one arrives in a city for the first time, the first thing one does, in order to understand its distinctive characteristics, is to explore the oldest neighborhoods and visit the buildings of greatest antiquity, which generally define the identity of a place and often provide a visitor with the most memorable experiences. In these historic sites, the city's original conditions and principles of identity tend to be revealed, manifesting, along with the topography and the climate, the most predominant manners of inhabiting the place. That is why cathedrals, sanctuaries, and civic centers are icons of identity.

These details seem not to make sense in Bogotá. In this city, a different logic prevails, and that is the remarkable thing about the Colombian capital: the possibility of reinventing itself and creating a contemporary idea of identity, unfiltered by its past and free of the burden of history. In the historic downtown, greatly modified, only the Catedral Primada and the Plaza de Bolívar show traces, to some extent, of the city's foundational era.

Perhaps the most singular thing —and what most clearly reveals the circumstances of the place— is not the cathedral, nor the historic neighborhoods and plazas, but a building that safeguards books

Rogelio Salmona
Bogotá, Colombia, 2001

and is at the same time an urban space, equipped with the infrastructure of a park, just a few kilometers to the north of the historic downtown. The park-and-building complex is just over twenty years old, but it clearly and consistently expresses the culture of the country, its aspirations, and its desires.

This piece of cultural infrastructure is the Biblioteca Pública Virgilio Barco, a public library that owes its name to a former Colombian president and the principal benefactor of the project. To my eyes, it is the most memorable building in all of Bogotá. This sanctuary cultivates a worship of both books and nature: its landscape and architecture are familiar to all residents of the Colombian capital, where the duality of metropolis and cordillera is ever-present. The library is sunk in a park, its great walls hiding it from the city and projecting it toward the hills and the sky.

Few contemporary buildings have succeeded so quickly in capturing and embodying the identity and ideals of a culture. It requires great civic spirit, political will, creativity, and capacity for synthesis to bring tradition, identity, and the cultural vanguard together.

Brick, the traditional material of the region, has been used in this complex with the same skill and affection as exposed reinforced concrete. The two constructive systems coincide in terms of radical geometries. The rooftops, also covered in red brick, are walkways and labyrinths in which it is possible to imagine a stroll over the clay tile roofs of the few old buildings that survive in the historic downtown, or atop the vernacular constructions of the Colombian highlands and parts of the Bogotá savanna.

The idea of the building is contradictory and at the same time complementary: nothing is wasted. Its ability to be at one and the same time both architecture and landscape, geometrical clarity and spatial complexity, a traditional expression of walls and an exemplar of great voids, artifice and nature, serenity and dynamism, endow this complex with a great variety of events, approaches, and experiences among its tranquil and silent contemplative spaces.

In addition to the quality of construction and the mastery of geometric design, evident in both the bonding of the brick and the lines of the formwork, the complex projects an image of avant-garde architecture, futurity, and local tradition. The time-honored tradition of extended wall surfaces is occasionally broken, allowing us to look ahead to open structures with skylights and to the park where traditional craft and the sophistication of contemporary logic coexist, where horizontality and monumentality are inextricably linked.

The Biblioteca Pública Virgilio Barco, by the architect Rogelio Salmona, is a surprising place: a cathedral of books that promotes from Latin America a hope in education, democracy, culture, and respect for the environment.

Salvador Macías Corona

5m

Section A-A'

0

30m

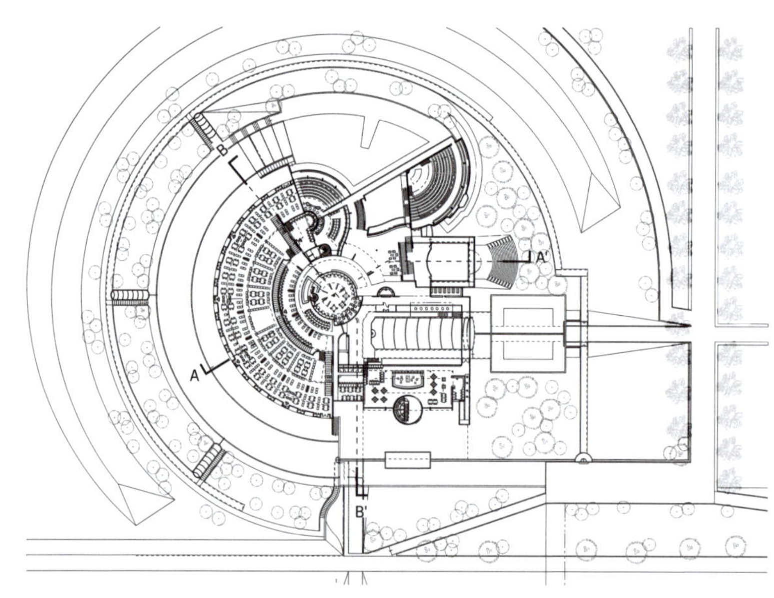

Level 1

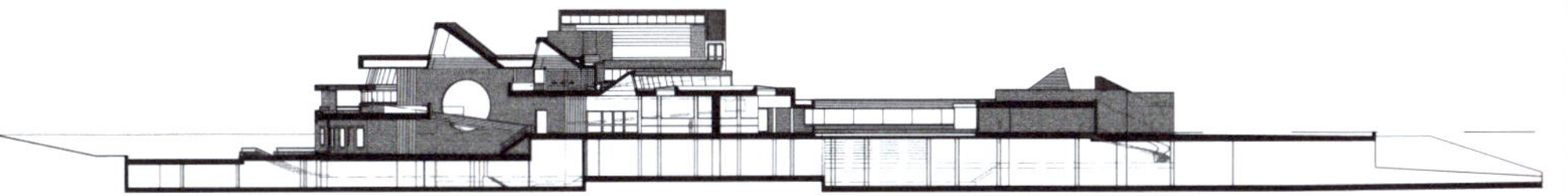

Section B-B'

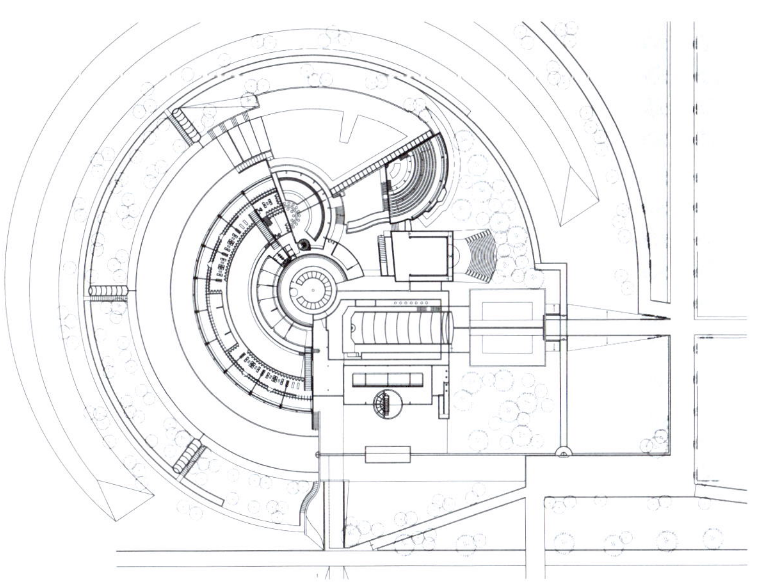

Level 2

Barco

Chapel of the Colegio Los Nogales

This early but mature work by Daniel Bonilla immediately received international recognition as one of the buildings that would mark the return of Latin American architecture to the world stage. The then-influential Emerging Architecture prize, awarded by the London-based *Architectural Review*, gave first place to the chapel and honorable mention to my own Casa Equis in 2002, which provided me with the opportunity (and the enormous satisfaction) to get to know Daniel personally. Since that time, we have built up a friendship that becomes more and more solid with every event in which we both participate, although we live on different continents. A visit we made together to the chapel a few years ago has encouraged me (and made it possible) to write about the work.

The chapel was completed in 2001. Entrusted with the design of a small chapel for a school in Bogotá, the architect submitted a design that effaces the limits of the commissioned construction, expanding it on a larger scale. Viewed in another way, it seems to propose the integration of the school space with the chapel. The roofed surface area is less than 370 square meters, yet the spatial arrangement orders and defines an area of more than four thousand square meters.

This is achieved through two strategies of different impacts and importance. On the one hand, the chapel embraces the adjacent

Daniel Bonilla

Bogotá, Colombia, 2001

space with elements that define an interiorized exterior. The use of free-standing walls and a reflecting pool that duplicates the building on a vertical plane creates a composition that we might initially associate with certain designs by Álvaro Siza. On the other hand, the chapel is located in an autonomous place. As with many successful projects, contingent circumstances led the architect to make unexpected decisions that lend a singular power to the design. During construction, the school authorities were uncertain about the ideal capacity for the chapel: one hundred or four hundred congregants. This was not the first time a chapel was expected to meet distinct demands. We might mention several examples of solutions to the problem of creating an intimate space for prayer, for celebrating a religious service for a small group of the faithful, and for receiving larger gatherings on other occasions. One of the most notable is the chapel of Notre-Dame du Haut in Ronchamp. Le Corbusier defined an interior space, but behind the altar, on the outside, he placed a second altar and pulpit facing a green esplanade, for masses with larger congregations on pilgrimage feast days. The concave and convex forms, which he himself described as "visual acoustics," allowed the interior chapel to be joined to an exterior one.

Daniel Bonilla responded to this contingency with a single space, of variable geometry, that allows the interior of the chapel to be used on both occasions, without doubling and with a great deal of flexibility. One of the sides of the nave is an enormous double door that opens onto a large green space, which becomes the center of the college quadrangle and the spiritual heart of the institution. The chapel itself is a pure, elemental prism, whose dynamic quality can be appreciated by how it lends itself to different rituals.

Opening the doors is a ritual in itself. If the congregation numbers more than one hundred, the chapel is opened by means of a collective action. The doors are so hinged that it is very difficult for a single person to open them, but easy if several people undertake the task at the same time. Common agreement is required.

The change in the liturgical axis, from the direction inside the chapel to one perpendicular to it looking out over the green esplanade, has been masterfully designed in all its details. Inside the chapel, the essential elements do not move, but they are adapted to a different use. When the doors open, the pulpit becomes an ambon; the presbytery space, a choir; and the chapel itself, a new presbytery, with its altar. Since the floor of the chapel is slightly higher than the ground outside, the tradition distinction is maintained between the elevated presbytery, where the altar is located, and the congregation at ground level.

The exterior esplanade has two types of ground: one hard and mineral and the other vegetal, with grass and trees. The former area, near the chapel transformed into presbytery, is contained and delimited by the bell tower, and has a capacity for four hundred congregants, as required. The latter area allows for even greater expansion and has frequently been used for gatherings of up to 1,700 people.

The added value of this flexibility in terms of capacity is flexibility in terms of use. The chapel, whether closed or open, can be freed of its religious purpose and adapted to gatherings of students and parents for social and cultural events, thanks to the recess that contains the doors, which creates a sort of porch or covered stage.

The materials, handled with precision and care, share in and reinforce this flexibility. Exposed concrete, pale ocher in tone, is used for the prism, with stone paving to signal the horizontal plane on which we walk. Wood is used for all the *movable* furnishings: not only the pews, but also the great doors, the protagonists of this mutability.

Jean-Pierre Crousse

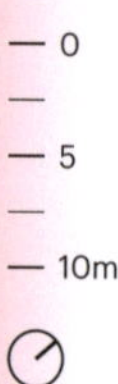

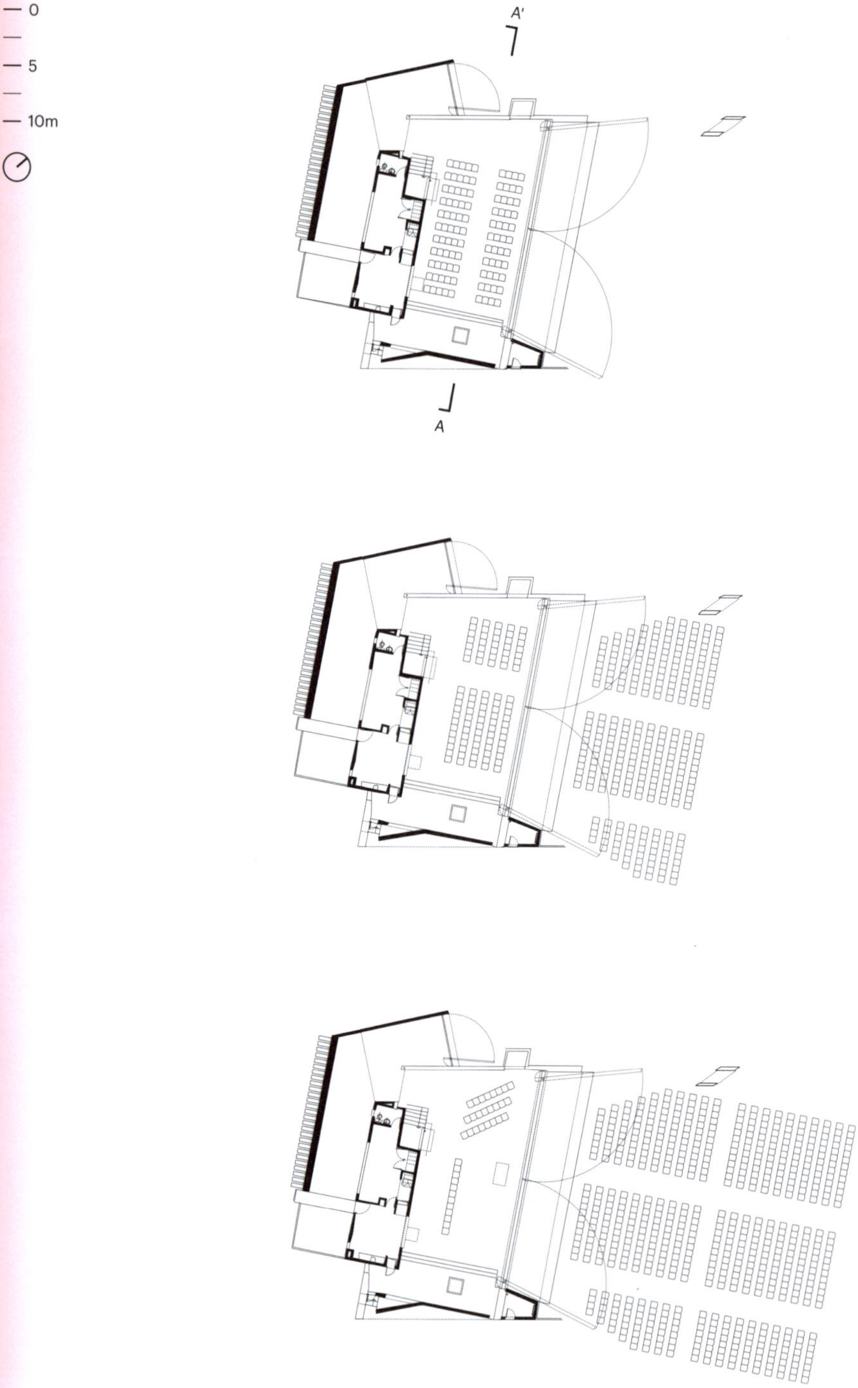

A'

A

Plans with different proposals for accommodation and capacity

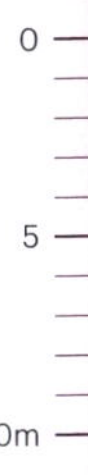

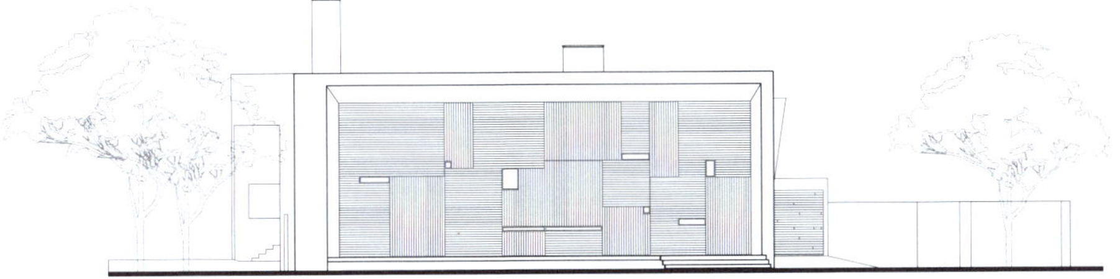

Elevation

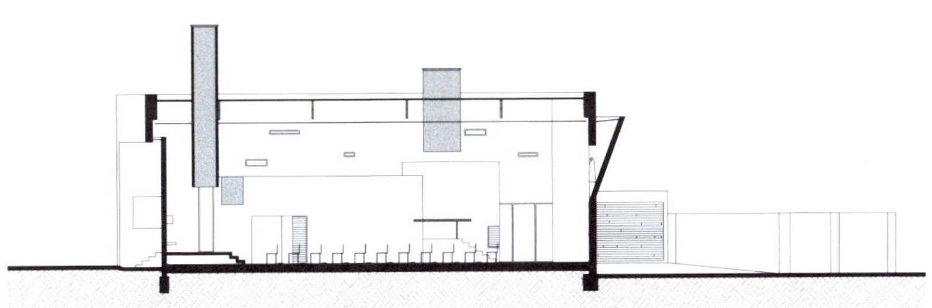

Section A-A'

Quinta Monroy

Abandoned

On a visit to chapel of the Capuchin convent in Mexico City, designed by Luis Barragán, the nun who was giving us the tour recounted some anecdotes about the building, underlining the respect she still felt for Barragán: "The architect wanted that piece there; the architect put this one here." I felt that, for the nuns, respecting each of Barragán's decisions somehow validated the experience and made it genuine. "All this is as the architect wanted it to be," she would say. Our guide also pointed out whatever was no longer in its original state, owing almost always to lack of funds. The reflecting pool in the central patio has a pump to keep the water in movement, so that its serene murmur can envelop the space: "The architect wanted the fountain always to be running, but the electricity is very expensive." Like the housewife of the Villa Arpel, in Jacques Tati's motion picture *Mon Oncle*, who turned on the fountain only for guests, the nuns turn on theirs only when receiving visitors.

When is a work finished? When the architect says so? Or is a work never finished, but only abandoned, as Leonardo da Vinci said? Barragán abandoned this work and left the nuns in charge of putting everything in its place (or failing to do so).

ELEMENTAL. Alejandro Aravena

Iquique, Chile, 2004

A few years ago, the Courtauld Gallery in London presented a small exhibition entitled *Unfinished*, consisting of works that artists either could not or did not wish to complete, and which therefore have gone down in history as "unfinished." In many cases we may wonder whether the actual intention of the artist might not have been to leave the canvas as we now see it, although their contemporaries were unable understand it. Most of the works were Impressionist in style: creations that forever transformed the notion of what a finished work is.

Quinta Monroy, a project by ELEMENTAL, is likewise an unfinished work, or a half-finished one. Abandoned. It is half-finished in order to allow it never to be finished, as with most uncontracted construction in cities in the developing world. The canvas is there; the rules of the game are there. ELEMENTAL proposes this series of rules. Form results from the strategy, which makes it possible that there be many architects over the course of time. This is not new. What is new in ELEMENTAL's approach is that the rules function with limited means: they serve the design and offer the freedom to go on.

This project touches on many issues. One is the personalization of housing: as in a computer, the hardware is the same for all, but the software is an individual choice. Each dwelling can be personalized at its own pace. The budget assigned serves to cover whatever is necessary on this checkerboard of possibilities. ELEMENTAL's approach raises the level of discussion about assisted or self-performing construction.

The project proposes the optimization of plans in order to create a common denominator that will allow for multiple possibilities. Each unit has a basic program: living room, dining room, kitchen, two full bathrooms, and two spaces for bedrooms. Expansion does not involve changing installations or putting in more bathrooms. The owner has only to insert an elevated platform or put up a wall in order to complete the spaces. In order to provide the owner with the possibility of rental income in the future, the dwelling can be divided in two, with entries on each level and a kitchen located where the installations are ready.

The idea is simple: the project puts up one wall and the resident puts up another. This makes it possible for new authors to be incorporated into a collective work, which is nevertheless controlled at important points. No one knows what the result will be, because there is no final result. Quinta Monroy is a work executed in four dimensions, so time needs to pass in order for it to be understood.

Francisco Pardo

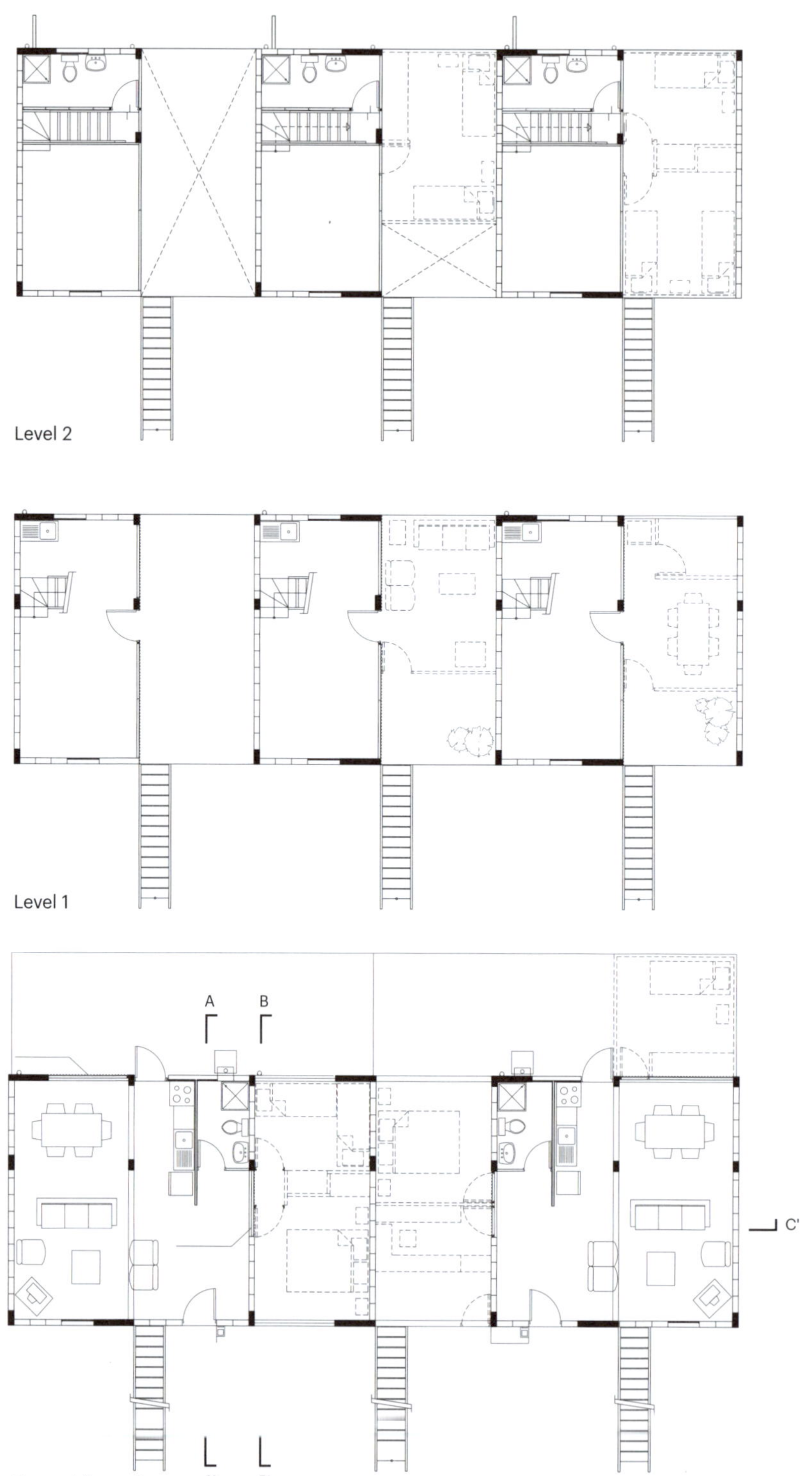
0
1
2m
Level 2
Level 1
A
B
C
C'
A'
B'
Ground floor plan

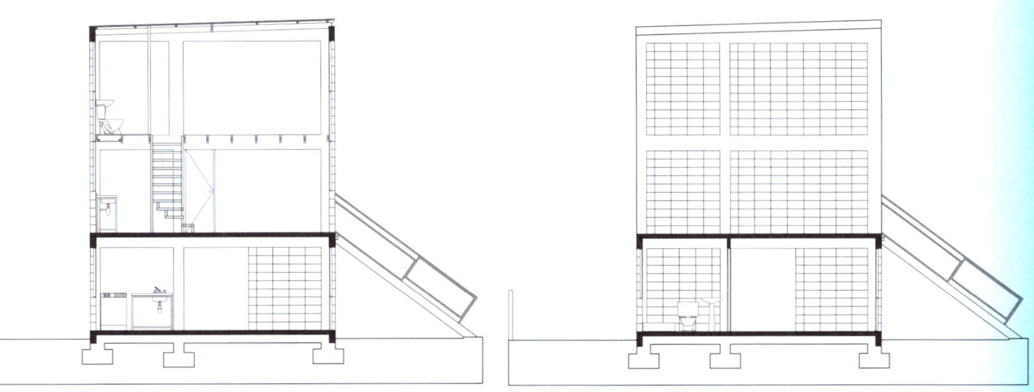

Section A-A'

Section B-B'

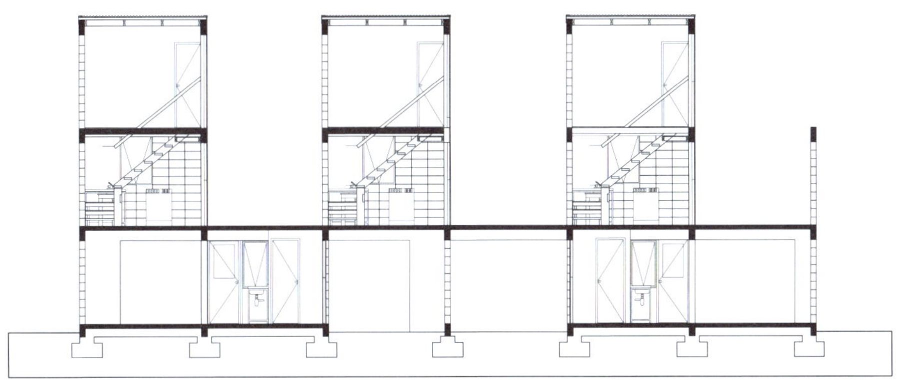

Section C-C'

Punta Pite

An irregular topography stretches along the Pacific Ocean, the waves breaking abruptly over the rocky coastline. In the course of natural cycles and the passage of time, the tides have shape a rugged geology and the seasons offer an ever-changing landscape. Punta Pite, in Zapallar in central Chile, is the most emblematic landscape project designed by Teresa Moller. Its potency resides in an interaction with natural forces, determined by the design itself. This is what artists like Robert Smithson aspired to do in their works of land art, creating variety out of reactions to the phenomena of the site.

The series of interventions into the rocky cliffside is part of the 11 ha private condominium, which includes several common-use and recreational spaces, such as the Headland Park, the Stone Path, the Cliffside Park, and The Pool, this last one of the most important in the complex.

The promenade begins, or rather ends, at the highest point. The residents reserved the Headland Park as a public-use space. The cluster of cypresses, treetops twisted by the wind, were already there, lending a surrealist air to the place. A former excavation associates water with the history of the site. The stones have been worked by Gerardo Ariztía as sculptural pieces that retain traces

Teresa Moller
Zapallar, Chile, 2005

of their rain-beaten origin, thus preserving the local memory of the place.

During the rainy season, water gathers in the concavities of the rocks or runs in a channel perpendicular to the stone path. The two axes intersect at the highest point of the site, forming a cross that seems to mark its foundation. Although the interventions are minimal, they orient the visitor both spatially and temporally, in the face of the immensity of the ocean and the notion of endless time.

The route along the cliff side interconnects, with the same poetic power, several spaces that dialogue with the existing landscape, while altering it as little as possible. The stone, quarried locally, was worked in traditional fashion by a team of local stonecutters, who translated the design aims *in situ*, as a response to walking the site, in the manner of landscape artists. Certain rules determined the design of the path: if a rock cut into the path, it was left exposed; the side facing the sea was cleanly cut, while the inner side shows uneven joints, depending on the contours of the terrain, as though the path were a line that does not seek visibility, but appears minimally and then disappears when necessary.

The stairways of the Stone Path offer the double opportunity of *touching* the landscape with the weight of one's body and the soles of one's feet. The horizontal and vertical movement connects the visitor with the topography by a complete sensory experience: body and mind in harmony with the tonality of the landscape.[1]
One monumental stairway stands out. Its exaggerated scale is not gratuitous, since it had to be striking in order to modify a context that was already powerful before any human intervention. The composition of the stairway recalls a great column with inverted entasis: by placing the spectator at the highest point, it achieves greater immersion on the landscape, generating an optical illusion, as the spectator's gaze seeks out the depths of the perspective toward the endless ocean horizon.

Teresa Moller has emphasized on numerous occasions the importance of bringing spectators and landscape closely together, in an intimate way. This notion has determined the width of the Stone Path, which can only be walked in single file. This offers users a "conversation with the sea," as she suggests, or simply a moment of solitary contemplation and quietude, for, as Jimena Martignoni has written, "the sea, with all its powerful presence, offers us silence."[2]
Indeed, the existence of silence is essential to certain landscape projects, such as Punta Pite, where the sea predisposes spectator to a certain mood, in close affinity with a dialectical landscape, which unfolds as a series of dualities: nature and culture, preexistence

1 The tonality refers to the mood provoked by the landscape: a spiritual tonality or atmosphere. In German, the word *Stimmung* designates the emergence of human feeling in the presence of landscape. See Georg Simmel, *Filosofía de paisaje* (Madrid: Casimiro Libros, 2013), p. 18.

2 Jimena Martignoni, *Reflexiones en el paisaje. Teresa Moller* (Mexico City: Arquine, 2021), p. 93.

and proposal, indefinite routes and clearly manipulated geometries, and so on.

Perhaps the finest expression of this dialogue is The Pool. As its name suggests, this is a concavity that collects incoming seawater. A rock emerges from the middle of the water, or remains submerged at high tide. At once sensitive and assertive, the landscape architect's eye configures a narrative out of this phenomenon. The rock has been modified by guest artist Aymara Zegers, who designed a new skin for the stone body out of bronze scales, marking its center with a vertical rod. The terraces that allow for human contact with the sea are laid out along this central axis, in order to delimit the void around the stone pavement, tracing the radius within which they dialogue with the rock in The Pool.

This rock is clearly a *hierophany*, a term coined by the Rumanian philosopher Mircea Eliade to designate a manifestation of the sacred. The rock interrupts the neutral and homogenous space of the sea. Its vertical axis marks a fixed center and indicates the intersection as a sacred earthly element that orients human beings in relation to the cosmos. The design is therefore a continuous dialogue between sublime nature and the subtle beauty of a landscape "where solid and liquid [have] lost themselves in each other."[3] At Punta Pite, stone and water coexist as an interdependent unity.

Andrea Soto Morfín

3 Robert Smithson, "El Spiral Jetty," in *Robert Smithson. Selección de escritos* (Mexico: Alias, 2009), p. 161. In 1970, the American artist Robert Smithson created his Spiral Jetty in Great Salt Lake, in Utah. Made of basalt, salt crystals, water, and mud, the work has been altered over the course of time by the fluctuations of the water.

General plan

0
5m

Orquideorama

Instructions for Cultivating Tropical Flowers

In the 1990s, following a period marked by the use of exposed brick and a professional practice focused on the development of housing, there emerged in Colombia, with the exemplary support of the municipal governments of Bogotá and Medellín, a new generation of architects with a vocation for public and urban space. The competitions sponsored by the aforementioned cities generated and democratized opportunities for many new architects to participate in the construction of Colombian cities, in the creation of a common life centered around public space.

The Orquideorama is an example of this generational change and of a new way of practicing architecture, with political and design positions closer to architecture understood as the construction of a philosophy, with experimentation as a way of operating. This new generations is prolific and full of ideas, which are summed up in this work.

Rather than a specific design, the project is a system composed of flower-shaped pieces or modules, which function by precise instructions to form a geometrical mosaic. I like to think that, rather than a "play of masses brought together in light" (in Le Corbusier's

AGENdA agencia de arquitectura + JPR Arquitectos + Plan:B Architects (with Alejandro Bernal)

Medellín, Colombia, 2006

formulation), it is a work of gardening. The flower modules are arranged in the botanical garden in Medellín and function as a vegetal ecosystem with a mind of its own. In a way, the Orquideorama has links with Fritjof Capra's writings about the study of life, with similarities to three of the conditions formulated in his book *The Web of Life*: 1) Life processes: actions and formal operations, the ability to tessellate and grow. Performativity: how to grow and adapt; 2) Form: pattern or organizing system-geometry: the flower-module (modulation, repetition); 3) Matter: the components and quality of the material: wood as an interchangeable material (elasticity/firmness). This is why I see the Orquideorama as a living system in a specific tropical context, which creates spaces of interchange and permeability between the different ambiences and layers of the place.

The construction is conceived as a plant species, even as it works for the plant species of the botanical gardens. This is one of the first approaches, perhaps, to conceiving of architecture in extra-human terms: an architecture for plants. It explores practices in which human beings are replaced as the only factor for defining the architecture, favoring concord between human and non-human agents. The program originally proposed in the competition was an exhibition space for orchids, but the open, modular character of the result has made it a multifunctional space, used not only for exhibitions but also a range of other activities: lectures, weddings, fashion shows, you name it... This has been achieved thanks to its indeterminate character and its integration with nature, where the physical limits between the construction and the surrounding vegetation is blurred. It is a place of climatic interchange between two worlds: the human world and the world of plants.

Another characteristic that makes the construction versatile and adaptable is its diagrammatic character, by contrast with specifically composed design models. Diagrammatic modular systems favor changes of program, challenging the idea that function is the only criterion for organizing buildings. The module as a typology allows for variations in use and organization, not only for human activities, but also for other agents, such as plants or animals.

If the Orquideorama operates as material strategy for cultivation —as I understand it to do—, it is therefore a material practice, with precise rules and protocols to mediate between the conditions of the site and the agents involved in it. Material practices work on matter and space in order to transform reality or their relation to the environment: they are involved in the behavior of systems —how systems act— and not only in their image and meaning. Gardening is one of these practices, and the Orquideorama is a flower garden.

In exploring the Orquideorama as an open system, rather than as a building, I wish to emphasize its ability to generate a material strategy aimed at growing, changing, and adapting to specific and temporary circumstances.

The Orquideorama exemplifies many of the characteristics of such systems: it is an unfinished structure, with the possibility of growing and adapting itself; it has no inherent scale or site; it challenges the notion of composition and favors that of configuration by arrangement; the program is interchangeable, based on rules and protocols that allow it function; it has formal and adaptive intelligence (like a living system); and it criticizes the idea of a specific object while favoring that of a field model (figure and ground).

I wonder what would happen if the Orquideorama were repeated in other places, so often that it were forgotten where it came from. We might imagine an architecture in which any architect could use the instructions and protocols to remake and recompose the modules of the original model. This would be the beginning of an architect-author who is not a single creator, but rather a promoter of processes, who seeks participative actions and generates ideas for co-creation, whose value resides not in the inspiration of the author, but rather in an open architecture that others can make and remake.

The rules and protocols produced by this anonymous architect would be the death of the author, as Roland Barthes understood it: a building does not belong to its architect, but rather to its co-creator and user. The disappearance of the signature author leads to the appearance of an author as agent, who acts and participates in a more communal way.

Flowers belong to everyone and no one. The Orquideorama sums up the notion of an open system: a relational building open to multiple interpretations, in which the authors are the strategists of a device.

Giancarlo Mazzanti

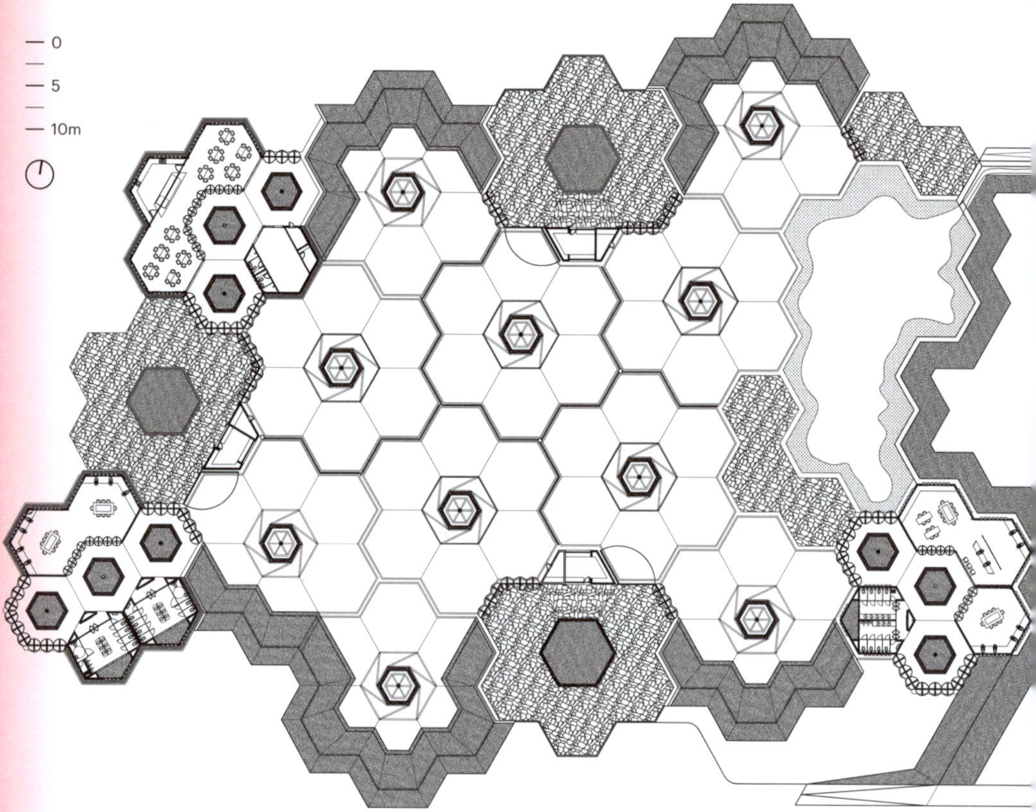

0
5
10m

General plan

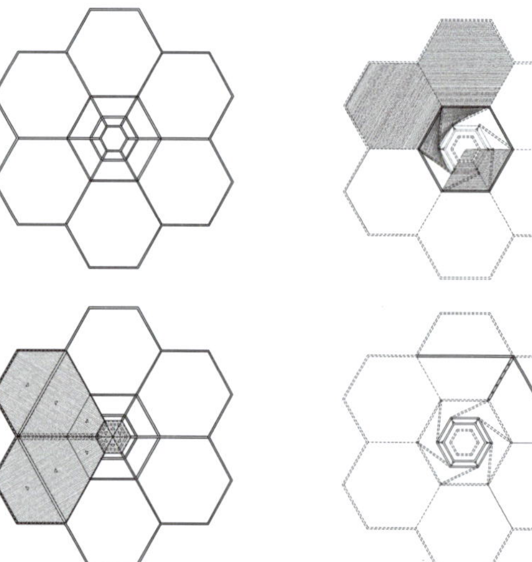

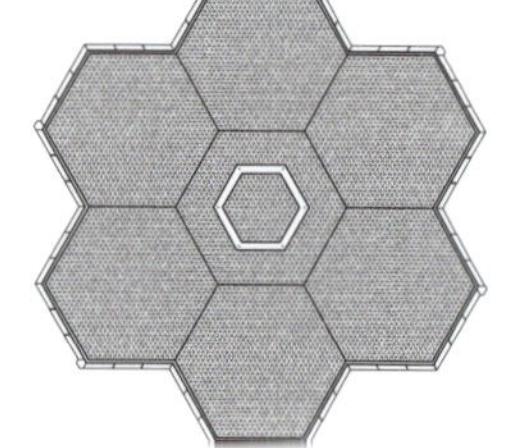

Typical floor plan

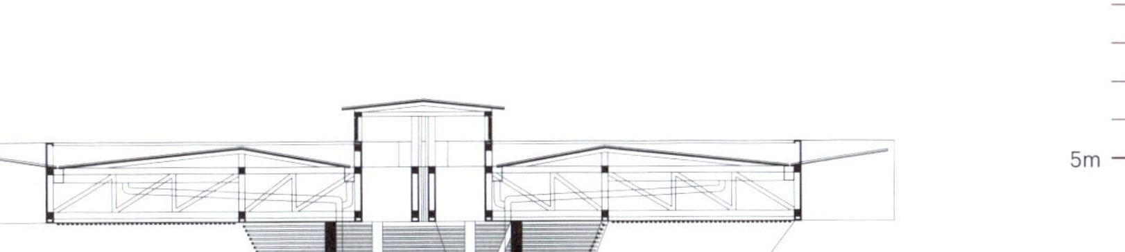

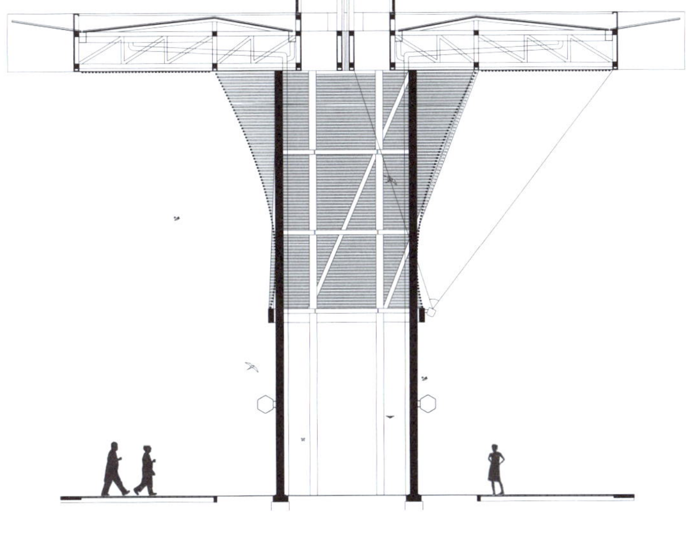

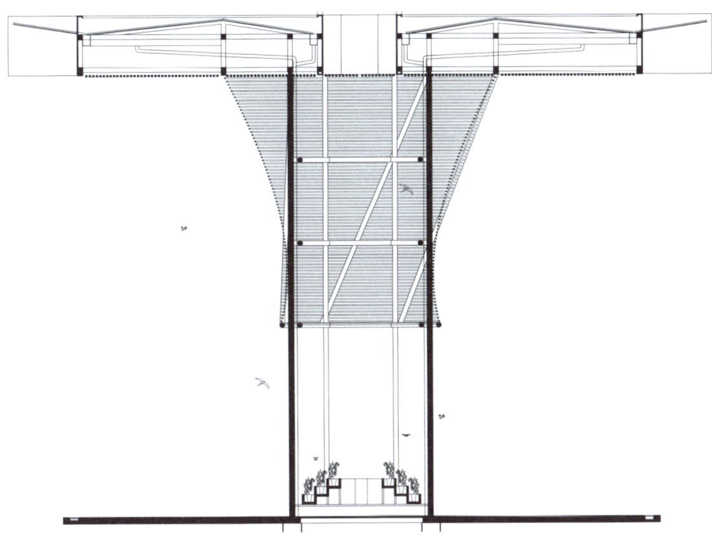

Sections

Biblioteca Vasconcelos

The Biblioteca Vasconcelos is at once spectacular and a spectacle. This winning design of an international competition fulfills a double mission as building and botanical garden. One might think that the symbiosis between nature and construction would relegate this cultural infrastructure to the status of a discreet urban event. The grand scale of the project, however, transforms it into a metropolitan element that articulates the areas of Insurgentes Norte, the Buenavista train station, and the Colonia Guerrero neighborhood. The project, intended as the central node of a national network or more than six hundred interconnected public libraries, embraced a sense of monumentality as a way of reaffirming the signs of its belonging squarely to its time and place, in a country with very low levels of reading.

This paradigmatic work, designed by Alberto Kalach in collaboration with Adriana León, Gustavo Lipkau, Juan Palomar, Emmanuel Ramírez, José Luis Reyes, Ignacio del Río, Enrique Rosas, and Tami Tamashiro, has its roots in Pre-Hispanic architecture and in some of the characteristic works of the Modern Movement in Mexico. The solemn and majestic central bay, the terraced platforms, and the wedge-shaped central stairways look back to both the Avenue of the Dead at Teotihuacan and the Ciudad Universitaria campus. The slanted planes recall not only the past of the Aztec capital, but

Taller de Arquitectura X. Alberto Kalach + Juan Palomar, Adriana León, Gustavo Lipkau, Emmanuel Ramírez, Tami Tamashiro, Ignacio del Río, Enrique Rosas, José Luis Reyes

Mexico City, Mexico, 2006

also some more recent architectural landmarks that turned to the same solution: the nearby Torre Insignia by Mario Pani, with its pyramidal form; the platform structures of Teodoro González de León and Abraham Zabludovsky; the terraced hotels of Ricardo Legorreta; and the Colegio Militar of Agustín Hernández, among others.

The plan of the building is a map of the library, a support for a cartography of knowledge. Like the great projects of the Enlightenment, it reflects an encyclopedic desire to understand and to order, in terms of both content and container. On the outside, the armadillo-scale cladding protects the reading rooms from direct sunlight, while still illuminating them. The saw-tooth roof plays both a formal and a functional role, flooding the large central space with light. The interior of the great shell of steel and concrete ribs is a spectacle all by itself. An enormous concavity, 250 meters long and 30 meters high, allows light to filter in through the slanted walls and the roof, from which clusters of bookshelves hang: Stereo structures —a term coined by Louis Kahn— that hold up spaces, analogous to hollow stones. Somewhere between the entrails of a ferryboat, the interstellar "space tug" of *Alien*, and the stalactites of Hans Poelzig's design for a great theater in Berlin, the Biblioteca Vasconcelos is at the same time quintessentially Mexican. Paradoxically, this colossal work connects with both pre-Hispanic monumentality and with emblematic works of modern Mexico (which also inspired the sets of the dystopian nightmare created by Paul Verhoeven and Arnold Schwarzenegger in *Total Recall*).

Timeless and schematic, like a sort of ruin, the building is indifferent to the fin-de-siècle trends that called for lightness, transparency, and smooth skins. The strength of its muscles can be perceived in the heavy walls, in the strain of the tensors from which the shelving hangs. The entire building can be seen from the serial spaces of the lateral reading rooms. The distinct identity of each room comes not from its own characteristics, but from its situation vis-à-vis the large central space that is the backbone of the library. Every element is subject to the same symmetrical rigor. As Rafael Moneo pointed out, as he toured the spectacular entrails of the Biblioteca Vasconcelos, the circulation areas —the great void— are in the forefront, while the reading rooms are subordinated to them, like appendices. The condition of these alveolar spaces is not so much to read as to be read. Their qualities derive not from the ergonomic dynamic that emanates from the space, or from the movements or repose of individual users, but from a greater, universal law: the entire design is in the transversal section. The stereometric definition of this thorax and each one of its successive ribs systematically resolve the conditions of the gigantic cavern. The great whale's belly of the Biblioteca Vasconcelos favors monumentality rather than intimacy. Indeed, it is not by chance that the skeleton of a whale salvaged from a beach in Baja California —a contribution by artist Gabriel Orozco— hangs in the middle of the enormous central space. It reconfirms the very essence of the great gallery, at once diagram and pleonasm.

An auditorium with seating for five hundred people and an informal reading area close out the central gallery space. The administrative offices are also off of the central spine, while complementary services are located at the back of the lot, in the independent structure of a preexisting industrial building, recycled as a greenhouse. The Biblioteca Vasconcelos has resisted the assaults of time and the neglect of several consecutive city governments, fulfilling its creators' initial promise to transform this new cultural infrastructure into "an ark bearing human knowledge, immersed in a lush botanical garden."

Miquel Adrià

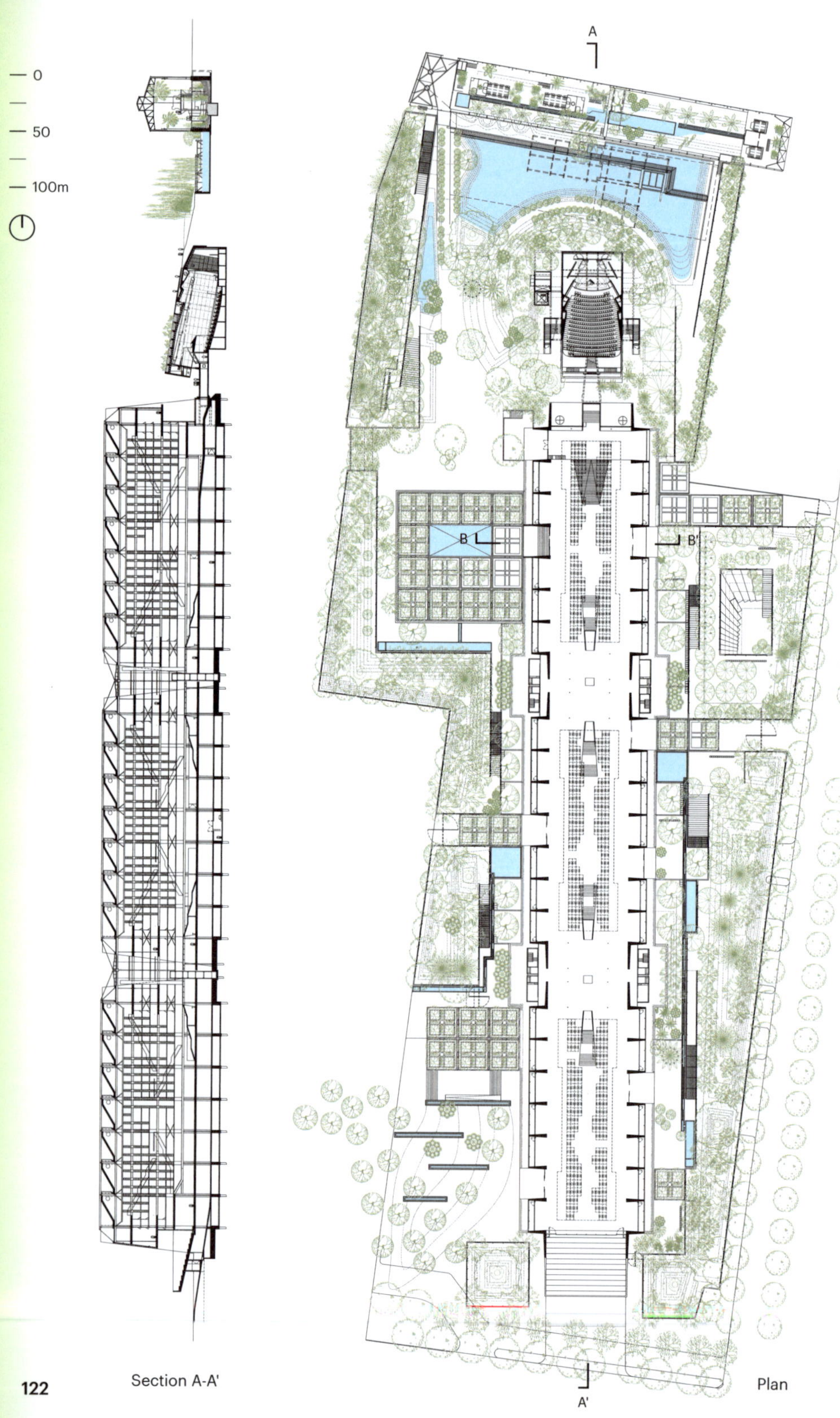

Section A-A'

Plan

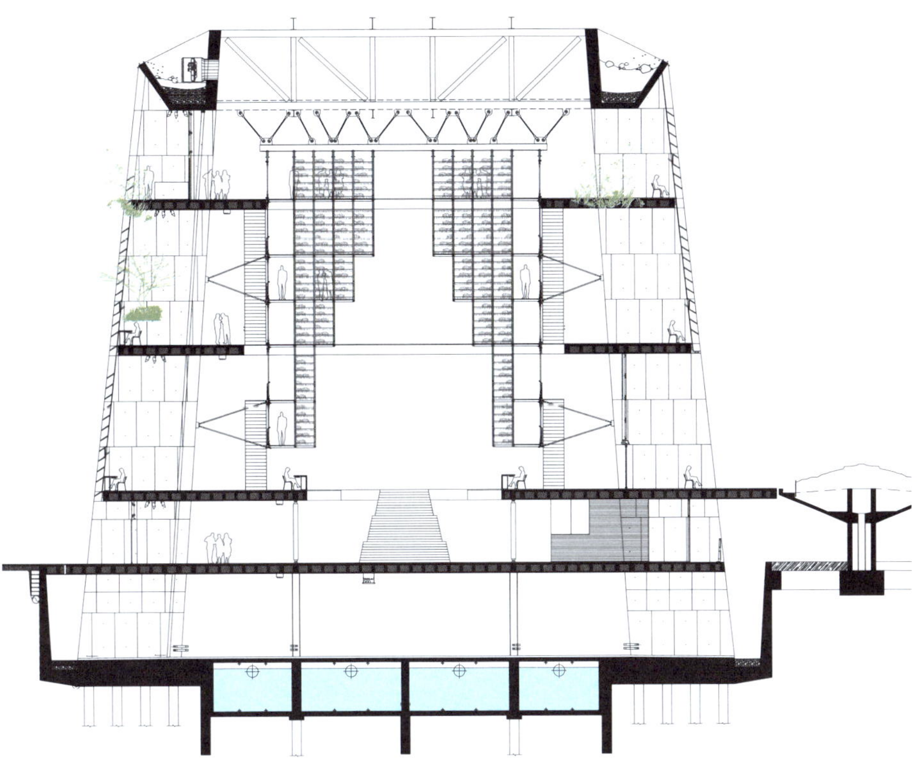

Section B-B'

860
860

LIBRERÍA
EDUCAL

800
920
800
800
700

650
370
340
340
330
330

Pabellones de Granja

Body, Matter, and Nature

The work of architects Mónica Bertolino and Carlos Barrado, of Córdoba, Argentina, functions in two essential directions: first it records imaginatively events and aspects of reality in drawings and stories, and then it gives material form, poetically, to these notations through housing, urban equipment, and public space. Their work opts for radical design, casting a different kind of gaze on everyday reality —rather like the short stories of Julio Cortázar—, and its principal aim is experimentation with forms and materials in relation with the environment.

An important part of their exploratory work consists of the workshops with students from around the world, which start with a mapping of the context and take into account the social, strategic, and sensory experience of the city. Mónica Bertolino also produces drawings and watercolors that address contemporary issues with irony and mordancy, focusing on Latin American circumstances and expressing a worldview that privileges creativity and harmonious coexistence. Her series entitled *Modulor contraataca* (Modulor Counterattacks, 1995-1997) is a critique of the machismo and Eurocentrism of Le Corbusier's drawings, while her collection of cows is an ironic commentary on Argentina's dependence on the livestock industry.

Bertolino Barrado Arquitectos
Córdoba, Argentina, 2007

The projects of the two architects draw on three basic concepts: an emphasis on sensory experience as the basis of an architecture corresponding to the scale and perceptions of human beings; an exploration of the possibilities of "archaic" techniques and materials, imbued with traces of an *arte povera* esthetic and allusions to archetypes —such as that of the primitive hut—, of recycling materials, of employing structural grids, and of reproducing organic and vegetal textures; and nature as a source of inspiration, with the creation of sensory landscapes as locations for their interventions, conceived as places to which architecture returns in order to be improved.

One of their most emblematic works is the group of educational farm pavilions sponsored by the gas station trade union within the natural reserve El 44, at the foot of the Urinorco, in Capilla del Monte in the province of Córdoba. The project was begun in 2003 and by 2008 two pavilions had been finished, one for the production of bread and sweets, and a second for housing animals. Placed at an angle within a natural environment, they synthesize the interest of Bertolino and Barrado in landscape architecture and its influence on them.

Nature is at the basis of the design. The pavilions are arranged at a right angle one to another, on different levels of the site. One runs along the more permeable border of the terrain adjacent to a line of fruit trees, while the other, which houses the animals, runs along the lower slope. Water is a protagonist of the design: it runs all around the perimeter of the project in the form of rectangular pools and runoff channels on the roof. In both pavilions, transparent walls allow the rocky landscape of the surrounding mountains to be enjoyed. The architecture absorbs and synthesizes certain classic concepts of the modern movement, such as the brutalist elements of Le Corbusier and the light, transparent pavilions of Ludwig Mies van der Rohe. Allusions to the work of Lina Bo Bardi and Paulo Mendes da Rocha can also be discerned.

These pavilions have been designed in accordance with the creationist method taught for decades in Córdoba by the architect and professor César Naselli (1933-2015) regarding the best way of handling forms, materials, and the incidence of natural light; they reflect the influence of the work of Miguel Ángel Roca, who collaborated with Louis Kahn in Philadelphia; and they clearly express the theoretical concepts of Marina Waisman (1920-1997), an unmistakable reference, with her emphasis on architecture as system, in relation to the context and historical structure of the environment.

There are many erudite notes and artistic allusions in the work of Bertolino and Barrado. In the pavilion for the animals, the concrete columns follow the rhythm of a musical score. The organic form of the ovens, alongside the more abstract volume, recall the cubicles for visitors at the entrance to the priory of Sainte-Marie de la Tourette, by Le Corbusier and Iannis Xenakis, as well as a performance with baking ovens by the artist Victor Grippo. The natural separations made with tree trunks recall the cactus hedge used by Juan O'Gorman to surround the houses he designed for Frida Kahlo and Diego Rivera in Mexico City. Numerous details of the pavilions also recall the braided world of Gottfried Semper, the organic structure of fractals, the abstract universe of rationalism and technics, and the poetics of works of art.

The work of Bertolino and Barrado is also illuminated by contemporary theory: the strictures on ornamentation and texture by Karsten Harries in *The Ethical Function of Architecture* (1997), which seeks to provide an ethical foundation for postmodern architecture; and the thought of Juhani Pallasmaa, as expressed particularly in *The Eyes of the Skin* (2005), which affirms that architecture is for all the senses, not just the sense of sight.

We can attribute to each of the pavilions an archetypal value. One of them is a "Platonic," a "Miesian" space, combined with the materiality of the architecture of Le Corbusier, in reference to the human ideal of pure, empty space, ordered and academic, configured by the glass panes which can be seen through but leave no trace on the senses. The pavilion for the animals, on the other hand, is telluric, half-sunken in the earth, its floor the ground itself. We therefore find a type of architectural work in which the context, everyday materials, and an appeal to multiple senses are revealed in all their primitive intensity. The pavilions constitute a synthetic lesson in architecture that is relevant —with artistic integrity and a connection to models from the past— to the context of the present.

Zaida Muxí Martínez and Josep Maria Montaner

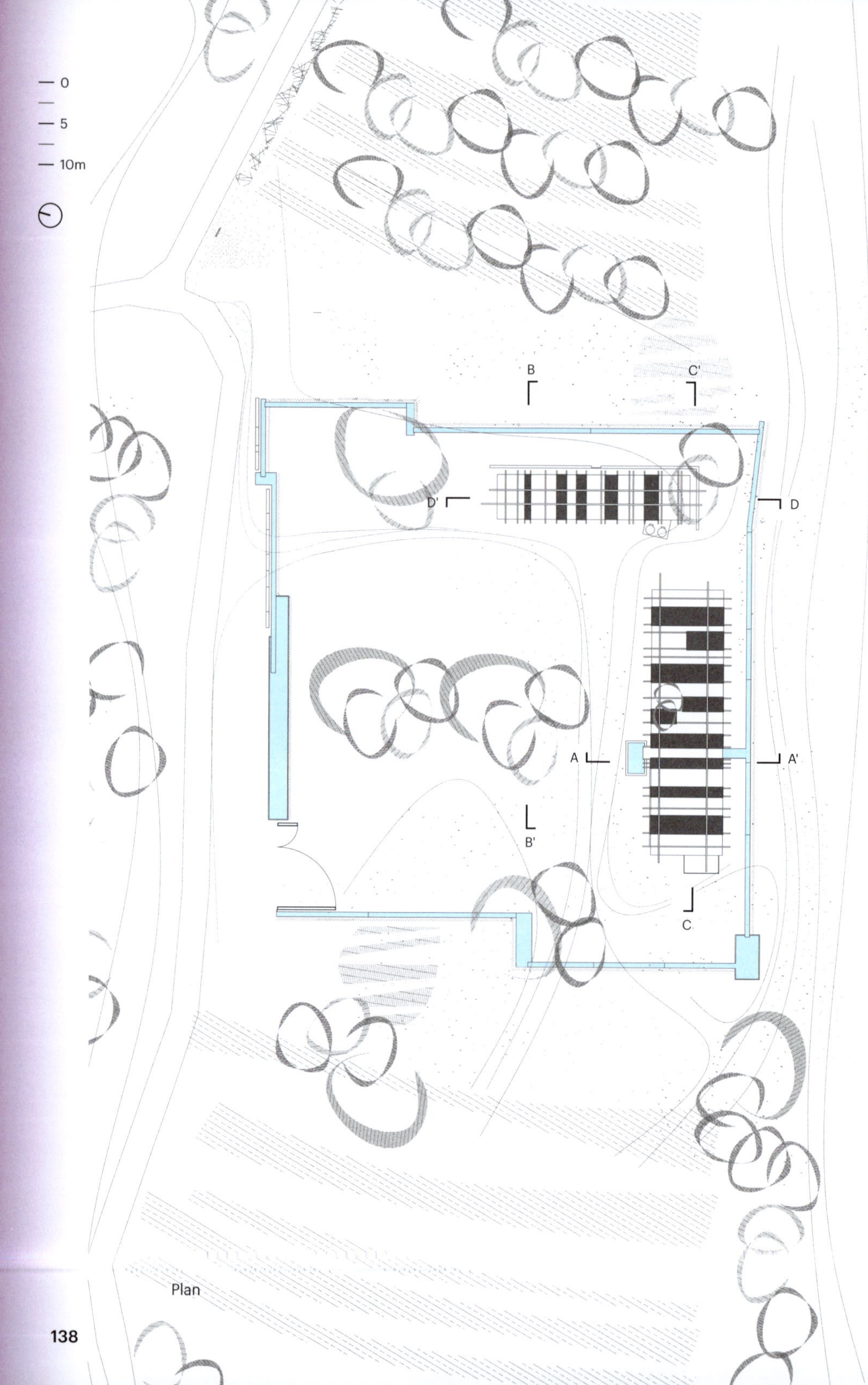

Plan

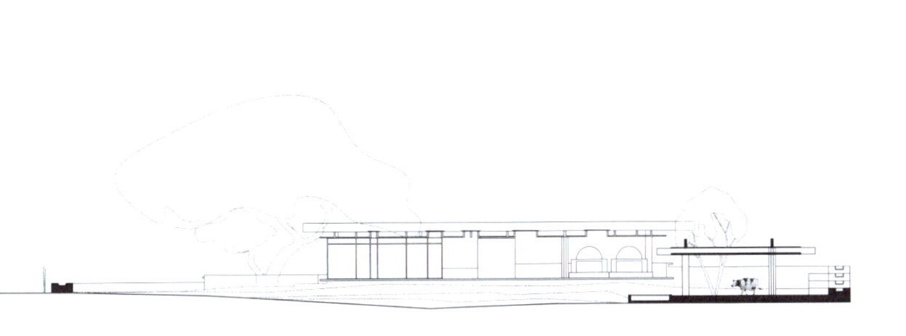

Section A-A'

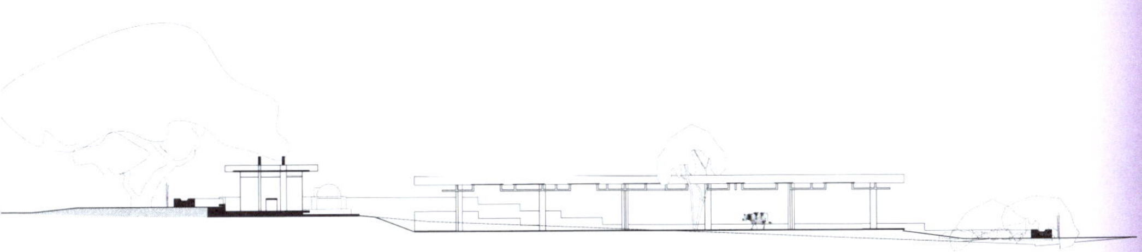

Section B-B'

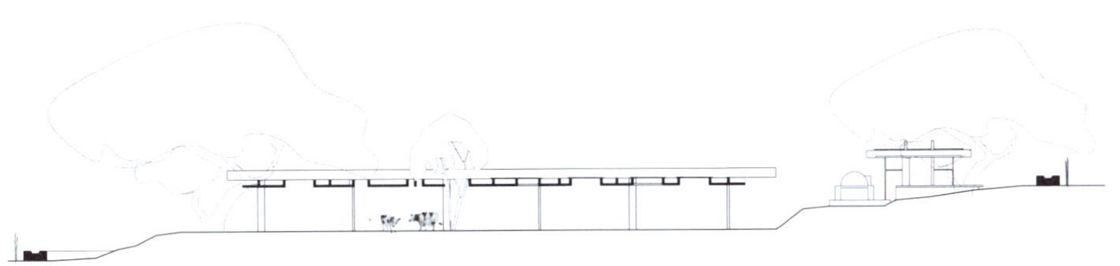

Section C-C'

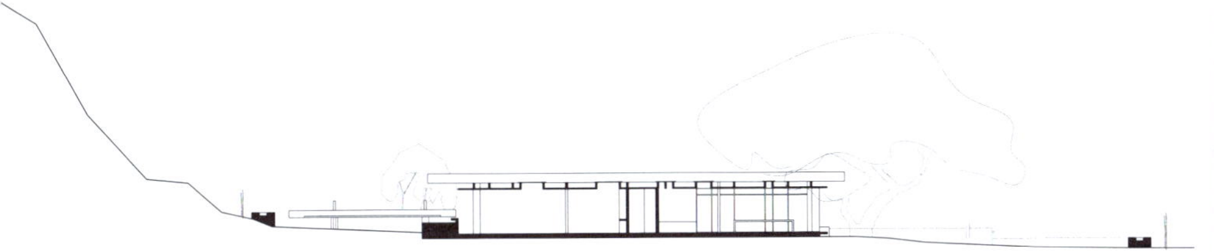

Section D-D'

Museo Universitario Arte Contemporáneo

What happened to the architecture of Teodoro González de León during the last twenty years of his career, until his death in 2016, with works like the National Conservatory of Music, the Paseo Arcos Bosques, and Museo Universitario Arte Contemporáneo (MUAC)? What happened to the city in which he lived, to his country and to the world in those last twenty-five years? Visiting the MUAC, an iconic work of the period, helps us to form an idea of his architecture and to answer our question. Mexican academic and cultural institutions, which, since the time of revolutionary era in the first half of the twentieth century, have mostly been state-sponsored, have favored venues and collections devoted above all to "nationalist" art and culture. In general, pre-Hispanic and colonial buildings have been relegated to the storeroom of history; the creations of independent and modern Mexico are piously catalogued; but it has taken years for architects and artists who abandoned monumentality or the revolutionary nationalism of the muralist movement to find a place in the public circuits of official culture, while the contemporary art of the turn of the twentieth century and beyond continues to find itself without sufficient exhibition spaces.

The MUAC was the university's response to this unfortunate omission, as it provided the first specialized venue in Mexico for those heterodox artistic expressions, difficult to classify within the

Teodoro González de León
Mexico City, Mexico, 2008

traditional division between the visual and performing arts. Ever since the construction of the Centro Cultural Universitario and the sculpture garden known as the Espacio Escultórico in the late 1970s, the campus of the Universidad Nacional Autónoma de México (UNAM) had remained intact, though it suffered from the budget cuts imposed by successive economic crises in the country. During all those years, no works of contemporary architecture had been built on the campus, except for a few modest and very clumsy interventions, and one or two discreet but more successful ones, such as the tower of the school of engineering, by Félix Sánchez y Asociados.

With the creation of the MUAC, the UNAM put itself in the vanguard as a cultural institution and completed its cultural complex with a museum devoted to contemporary art. The choice of Teodoro González de León for the commission could not have been more fortunate. His experience in museum design, his wide esthetic culture, and his skill in handling public spaces were a guarantee of success. It might be added that the university was repaying a long-standing debt to the architect, who had collaborated without credit, as a student, alongside Armando Franco, on the original competition-winning design for the campus.

There was no shortage of voices opposed to the intervention in an environment so rooted in recent history as the landscape of the university campus, which had been reserved for years to certain powerful architects, who lacked the youthful vigor demanded by new generations and new artistic expressions. Upon receiving the commission, González de León set off on a world tour of contemporary art museums. As he relates in the journal of his first trip to Japan, at the age of seventy-nine, accompanied by his companion Eugenia Sarré and his local hosts Montserrat and Aurelio Asiain, he visited the 21st Century Museum of Contemporary Art, Kanazawa, designed by SANAA. He described his visit in this way: "The museum is surprising, perfectly executed, fresh and not at all solemn. Highly complex simplicity."[1] This visit to the building designed by Kazuyo Sejima and Ryūe Nishizawa must have made a deep impression on González de León: much deeper than is evident from the few lines in his travel journal, because reminiscences of the Japanese museum in the MUAC are inevitable.

Using a few precisely focused strategies, he inserted the new museum into its context, which seemed to be awaiting the intervention in order to be complete: a plaza covers up a barren parking area; the entrance to the museum is aligned with the axis leading to the Sala Nezahualcóyotl concert hall; and an inclined glass façade, seventy meters long, overlooks and contains the plaza, with a striking ease that reflects the strength and refinement of the building's interior.

The plan recalls that of the museum in Kanazawa, but also calls to mind the legendary labyrinths of Aldo van Eyck: "Separate rooms of different dimensions and heights, communicated by a labyrinth of white corridors, illuminated by four patios."[2] The words seem to describe his own building. Inside the museum, one seems to be

1 Teodoro González de León, *Viaje a Japón* (Mexico City: Arquine+RM, 2006), p. 21 [entry for 1 June 2005].

2 Ibid., p. 21.

walking around a little city, with avenues, plazas, parks, and buildings. It is strikingly Japanese in spirit, not so much by its form as by its connection with gardens and patios. One goes in and out of the spaces as in scale-model metropolis, which might be compared to the Museo Tamayo, where the museum spaces are barely distinguishable from the circulations.

In the years between the Centro Nacional de las Artes and the MUAC, González de León freed himself of his penchant for ornamentation and a certain rhetorical treatment of his materials. The latter museum is pure space and light. It does not use bush-hammered concrete which, in additional to lending a more vernacular character to the volumes, concealed the defects of an industry unwilling to modernize itself. Here the material seems raw, uncooked: fixtures and moldings disappear, along with anything that "spices up" the material, as in Japanese cuisine. The space and the light are both resplendent. The elaborate and very successful solution for reflecting light into the exhibition rooms —invisible to visitors except by its effect— is impeccable, and underlines the nudity of the space: "Natural light brings out the thousands of works concealed in every work."[3] It is not surprising that Teodoro traveled to Japan four times in eight years, between 2005 and 2013. He had never before visited this luminous country, but the world itself was now more ductile and long-distance communication was at the speed of light. Japan, as no other place, synthesizes this coexistence of accelerated hypermodernity and the perennial repose of light, shadow, and silence in its Zen gardens. It is this double sensation of contemporaneity and timelessness that the luminous galleries and patios of the MUAC transmit as one walks again, years afterwards, along its corridors.

Ernesto Betancourt

3 Teodoro González de León, *Viaje a Japón II* (Mexico City: Arquine+RM, 2012), p. 69.

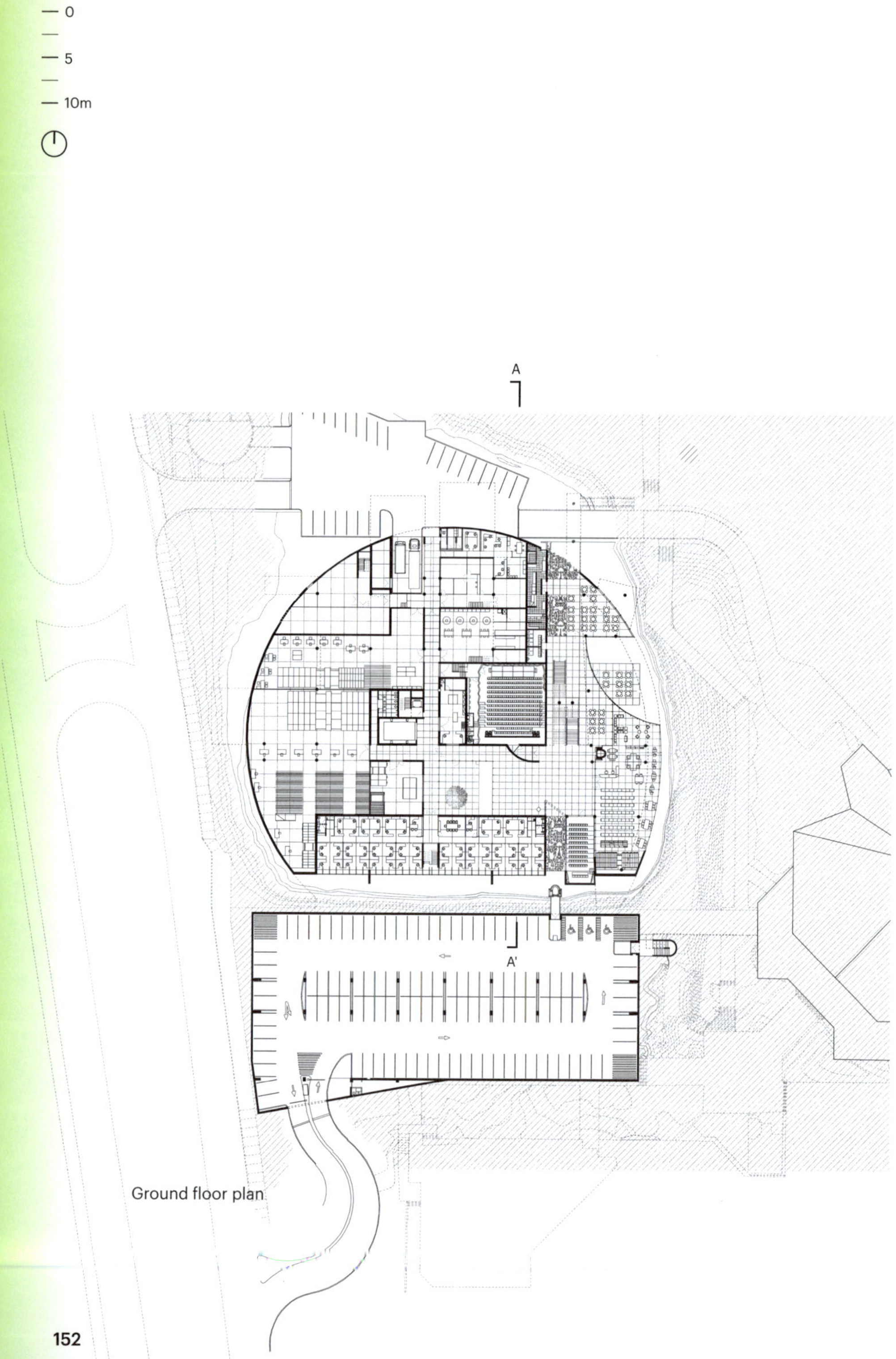

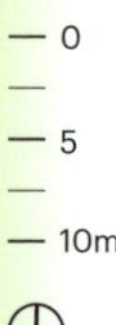

A

A'

Ground floor plan

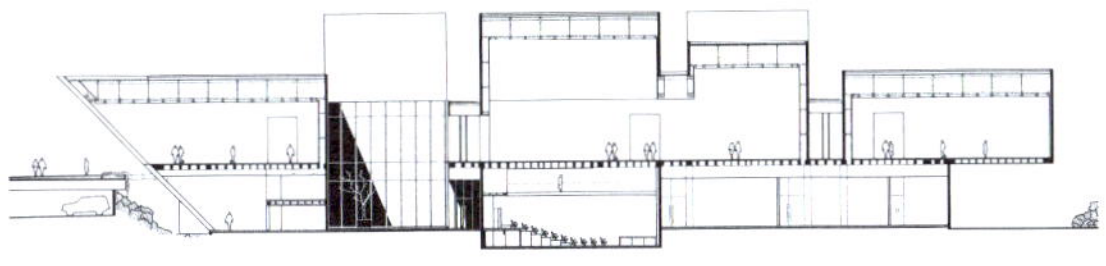

Section A-A'

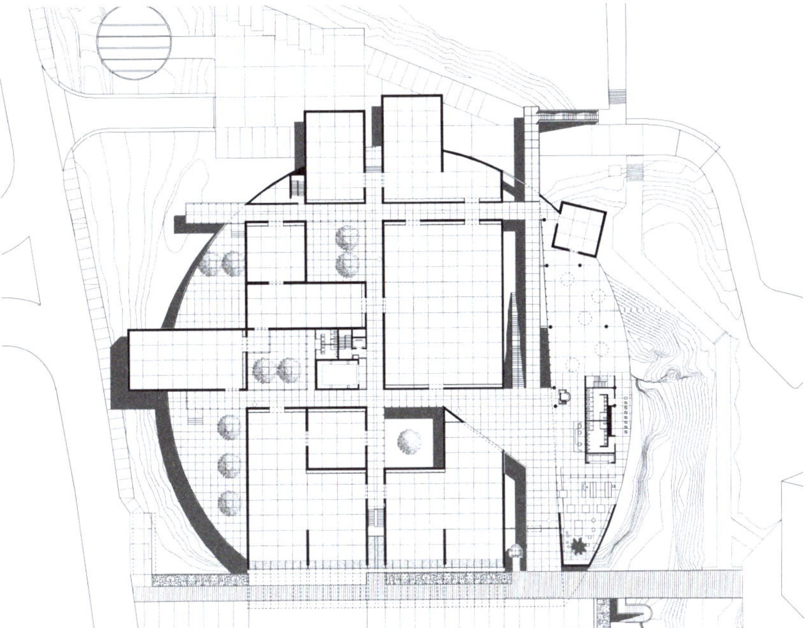

Upper floor plan

Fundação Iberê Camargo

The Stone Raft

In *The Stone Raft*, José Saramago's 1986 novel, the Iberian peninsula comes mysteriously detached from the European continent and floats into the Atlantic, like an island halfway between Europe and the Americas, thereby creating a new spatial, cultural, and geopolitical interrelationship. Of its detachment from Europe, it can only be speculated that Joana Carda, one of the novel's protagonists, traced a line on the ground with an elm branch, marking off a here and there, an inside and an outside, with a gesture of belonging and absence. After that, nothing was ever the same: even dogs who had always been quiet began to howl.

Like Joana Carda, Álvaro Siza first traced lines in his inseparable notebook, and then on the site itself, in solid concrete. He created another stone raft that has moved the present, the future, and the history of architecture on both sides of the Atlantic, reestablishing a conversation in the discipline between faraway places, which perhaps went unnoticed at the time. Very few took notice or offered interpretations; and unlike the dogs in Saramago's novels, we are just now starting to bark.

Álvaro Siza

Porto Alegre, Brazil, 2008

Siza deliberately brought the two worlds together in his 2008 design for the headquarters of the Fundação Iberê Camargo in Porto Alegre Porto, Brazil. Coinciding and interrelated in the work are Europe and the Americas, Portugal and Brazil, past and present.

By revisiting the process that led to *The Stone Raft*, we can perhaps identify the effects of Siza's project. Bold lines and detachment, outward voyage and return, materiality and change are keys to an explanation of why the home of the Fundação Iberê Camargo is one of the most representative works of architecture in the last twenty-five years in Latin America. Let us begin at the end, outlining the lessons and opportunities provided by Siza's project.

Generalizing a little, we might affirm that architecture in Latin America is most frequently practiced by architects who work with complete geometrical pieces and shapes, unequivocal figures, easily recognized in terms of volumetric form, supported by materials of a character halfway between industrial and vernacular, doubtless based on an academic tradition and manner of working derived from critical regionalism. The result is works of a markedly tactile quality. Most of them, when explained by their creators, manage to be categorized discursively in a rather superficial phenomenological vein, but the architectural programs generally fit into a container with no waste of space. The critical gaze is absent, distracted by notions and commonplaces typical to these geographies, such as texture and object, which reduce the production of architecture to a few easily classified characteristics.

In the case of the Fundação Iberê Camargo, Siza works in a different way: he places the elements under tension and asks questions before seeking certainties or conclusions. In this tension he points out other ways of doing and thinking about what is most immediate, drawing on the resource of the interpretative imagination, which allows for many readings at many times: in other words, it starts a conversation rather than constructing an opinion or formulating a conclusive argument.

In his design, Siza turns to the forms of modern Brazilian history and their global effects, like an open encyclopedia. By interpreting them in the light of the present, he makes us doubt the influence of European modernity and ask ourselves whether the construction of that modernity was purposely implemented in his own interpretations of the modernizing promises of Brazil. He even makes us suspect that modernity was a Brazilian invention, and that its own radicalism and inventiveness helped to spread it around the world.

Siza plays with the rules of the game. He knows them, and he breaks them, inviting us to participate in a different direction. In his invitation he reveals another path, focusing not on the obvious, the immediate, and the simplified, but on the elaborate. He shows us that architecture is dialogue and confluence. When Siza is around, he invites other voices to join in, and reminds us that Lina Bo Bardi, Le Corbusier, and Oscar Niemeyer are all in Brazil, in ramps, curves, and perforations, connected perhaps by the common thread of materiality. Siza opens our eyes and enables our practice in unusual ways, working with painstakingly selected fragments that acquire coherence in the memory of visitors and other architects as spatial experience. He is also a living witness to his own encyclopedic knowledge and skill, to a know-how that has become ever scarcer. He looks back in order to leap forward, guided perhaps by Walter Benjamin's angel of history.

With subtlety and sophistication, Siza leads us construct a dynamic context, which tends again to throw in doubt modern certitudes and regionalist ingenuity. Out of architecture itself, he constructs a different relationship with what we have been taught as truth or history: in other words, he creates a different present, using architecture as way to narrate facts, encounters, and interchanges.

Siza interprets history and the context by inviting other architects into his work, not as literal quotations, but rather as products of his imagination and erudition. Without falling into an abuse of iconography, he carefully selects and takes up scattered fragments of "guest" architects. Accepting the strain and complexity that his decisions entail, he presents architecture not as a collection of stable figures, forms, and spaces, but from an opposing viewpoint, far from superficial phenomenology or ingenuous regionalism. Siza presents us with a radical, monolithic, concrete vessel, anchored between thoroughfare and sea, which eludes any obvious reactions. He invites us to imagine a different history: he points out a different path, a journey constructed with time, material, and space, not one conceived simply as phenomenology or overworked contemporary media hype.

The building is configured by four pieces. Three are low volumes, organized as a sort of collage and contrasting one with another, interconnected by means of the empty and residual spaces produced by their articulation, resulting from the amorphous cuts and subtractions from the masses of these base volumes. This operation establishes a sense of coherence and continuity among the constituent parts, constructing a whole not from solids, but out of voids. The series ends in a higher fourth volume, which immediately commands the attention of anyone observing the composition. Here, the circulations between floors, which would normally be found inside, in a marginal space, are on the exterior: the most striking characteristic of the design. These three ramps are independent one of another and detached from the slightly curved higher volume. This gesture, supported by means of beams to the main structural nucleus, suggests that Siza is building a unity out of memories and desires. Although these do exist in terms of material continuity, associated with that of the volume that sustains them, at the same time they project a sense of absence, of something missing. Since we do not know what this is, we are forced to imagine how to fill in the absent pieces without the support of materiality or an episodic phenomenological effect (typical of made-for-Instagram contemporary architectures), and rather by means of materiality itself.

Materiality is only the vehicle by which to establish its ambiguous condition in our understanding of the whole, abstract and literal, referential and autonomous. The absence of matter, outlined by the voids between volume and organs, cannot be read in the union of the pieces, but rather in the tension between them, for even without touching, they interconnect. In their condition as beam/bridge, as circulation/volume, they constitute elements that only fit coherently with the rest in plan view, by connecting with the low volumes described above and forming a series of small volumes and cracks which suggest slight fissures by which to manipulate the mass. In this way, each piece expresses itself freely, but without losing any sense of unity, suggesting complementary geometries shaped by the void.

There is nothing new about the elements that first capture our attention in Álvaro Siza's building for the Fundação Iberê Camargo. We recognize many of them because we know where they come from, but it is through the sum of the parts and his way of articulating them (perhaps the only constant feature of Siza's work) that this whole is redefined and becomes something new. The individual elements, which did not seem new to begin with, become so in a new whole.

We are witnessing a new way of practicing architecture, one that is difficult to imitate. Siza's architecture speaks of many architectures at once. Their synthesis shows that, in order to explain and learn from the Fundação Iberê Camargo, only an oxymoron such as Saramago's (a raft that is of stone) shows the way to establishing other narratives. Stone rafts have to keep moving: otherwise they sink. Siza's design obliges us to move, not only in physical terms, by way of the ramps, but also in procedural ones, for its invites us to detach ourselves from the obvious, from the languages we have inherited from our phenomenological education and perhaps an oversaturated critical regionalism. Perhaps both the procedural and physical aspects come together on this stone raft, inviting us to move about and look out through the few windows at the endless ocean horizon, in order to see that history is fluid, graspable, and transformable. As Siegfried Giedion put it so well: no one touches history without transforming it.

Camilo Restrepo

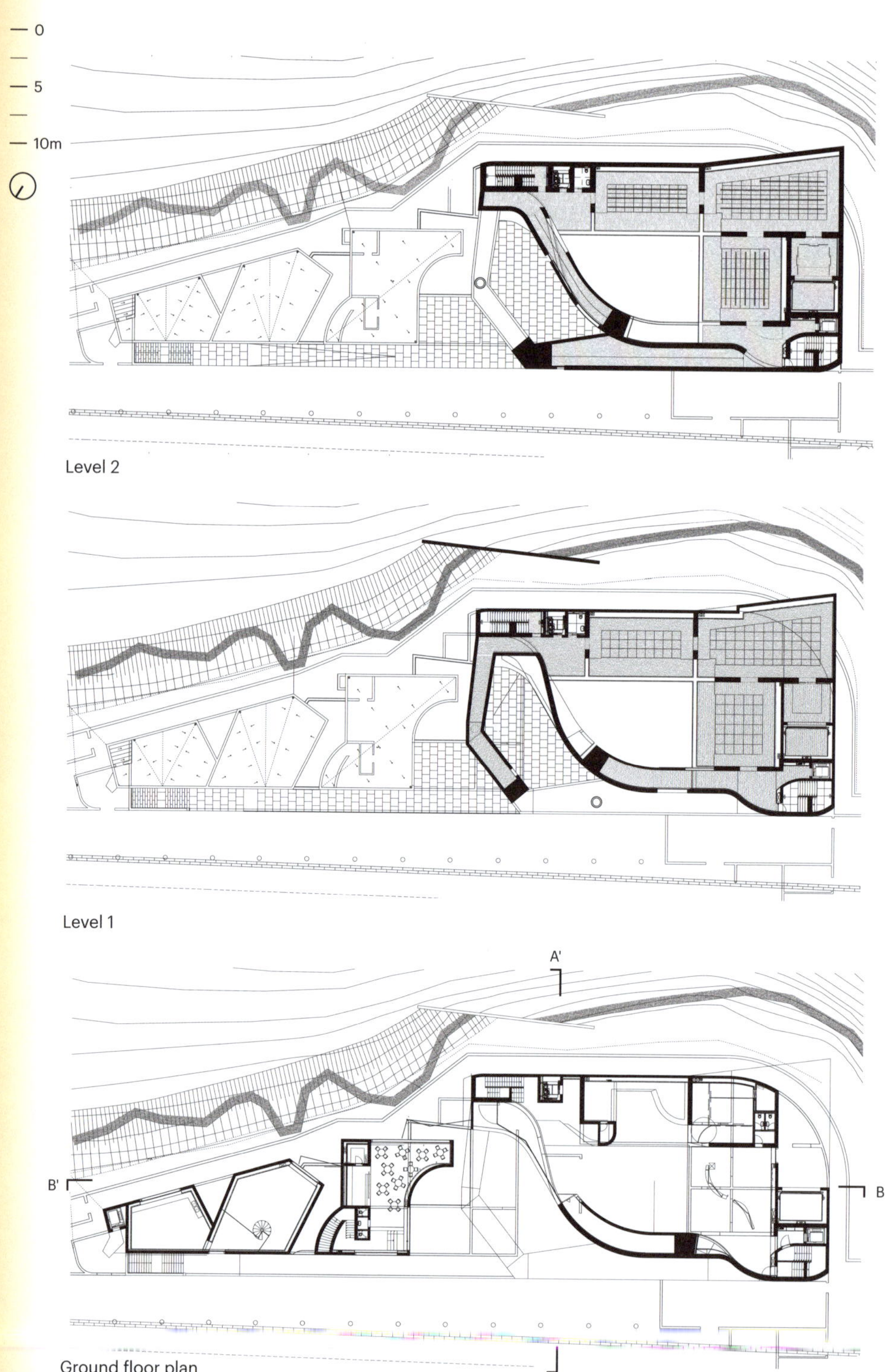
0
5
10m
Level 2
Level 1
A'
B'
B
Ground floor plan
A

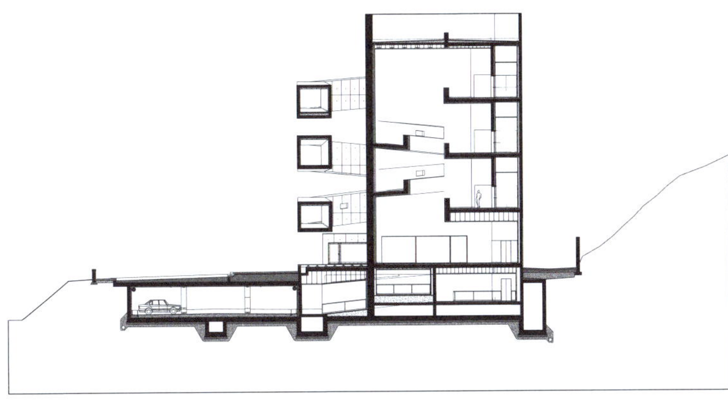

Section A-A'

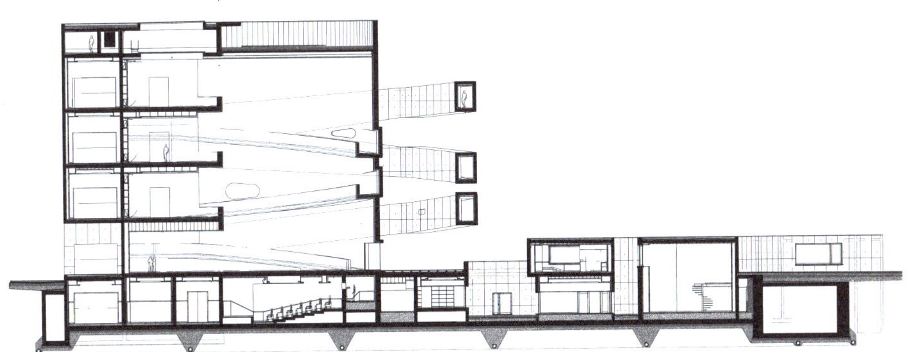

Section B-B'

Álvaro Siza

IBERÊ CAMARGO
IBERÊ CAMARGO

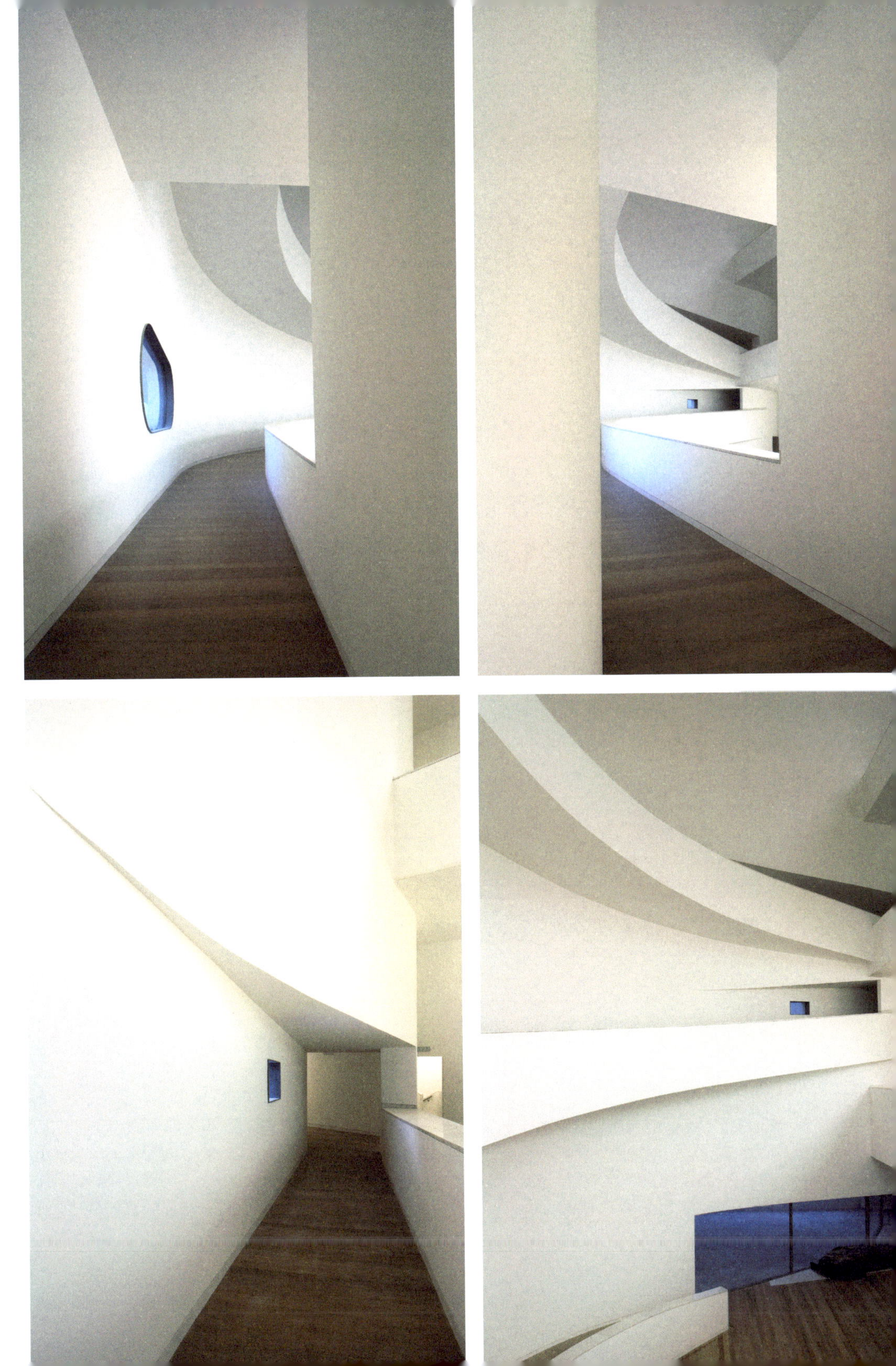

Termas Geométricas

What makes for exceptional architecture? In my opinion, it has to possess certain features and attributes that make it able to move us, to provoke sensations, to leave us with significant images and memories. This is what I experience every time I visit the enigmatic architecture of the Termas Geométricas, a hot spring complex that Germán del Sol has constructed near Coñaripe, along a ravine on the slopes of the Villarica volcano, in the lake district of southern Chile.

Before the intervention, the site was wild and virtually inaccessible. The hot springs emerge naturally at various points in a landscape full of rocks, trees, moss, ferns, and giant rhubarb. I am sure that Germán del Sol laid out the striking geometrical route of the walkways with stakes and stretched cords, and that the veritable design began with a reformulation of the work as a whole. He is sure to have molded the place with his own hands and those of the workers under his direction. The finished product was the result of errors, corrections, accurate estimates, and adjustments to his initial ideas, which enabled him to define with intelligence the arrangement and geometry of the walkways, thermal baths, terraces, changing rooms, and the thatch-roofed cabin, or *quincho*.

To my understanding, this is in a way a self-taught architecture, intentionally free of preconceived rules and canons. It is a manner

Germán del Sol

Coñaripe, Chile, 2009

of construction that evokes something primitive, enriched by the very austerity of its limited materials: mainly wood, stone, and reinforced concrete. It is a sort of taming of the natural landscape by means of architecture and the construction of an experience. Moving about the Termas Geométricas, one finds oneself in an atmosphere permeated by steam, humidity, the fragrances emanating from the forest, and sound of running water. Through this misty veil, the architecture dominates every part of the ravine, its presence accentuated by the contrast between the red and black of the constructions and the natural chromatic palette of the forest.

The extensive walkway-ramp invites visitors to undertake a zigzagging exploration of the ravine. Below, a conduit supplies the pools with hot water and keeps the planks warm and dry enough to make walking on them safe and enjoyable. Twenty or so isolated hot pools offer a certain degree of privacy, safeguarded by the distance between the different pools and the protection of the rocky slopes of the ravine. Changing rooms are scattered along the route and the *quincho* marks the entrance and exit from the complex.

Germán del Sol's projects frequently draw on ancient practices and traditions, with references to architectures of remote eras and anonymous architects. The walkways, the water mills and conduits, the changing rooms and the *quincho* are all reminiscences of the vernacular building practices of southern Chile.

The Termas Geométricas attest to Germán del Sol's lucidity, his ingenuity, and his well-supplied stock of architectural references. In my view, it is his instinctive resistance to fashions and trends that render his architecture so free of prejudices and special interests. The hot spring complex seems to be a timeless place, which may have already existed there for many years, lost in time. No deterioration of the installations is evident, in spite of their being exposed to the elements and to the wear and tear of daily use. The management undertakes routine maintenance to prevent any deterioration: wood is replaced, the pools are repaired, and surfaces are repainted.

I would like to think that this architecture will survive without any loss of those attributes that make it unique and unrepeatable. I trust, moreover, that it will be one of those few constructions that several generations are able to enjoy, that it will persist over time as a clear image and exceptional reflection of the architecture that Germán del Sol has bequeathed to us, as an exemplar of the material culture of our time.

Cristóbal Molina Baeza

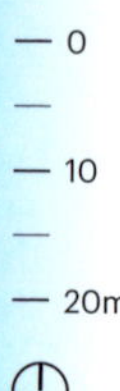
0
10
20m

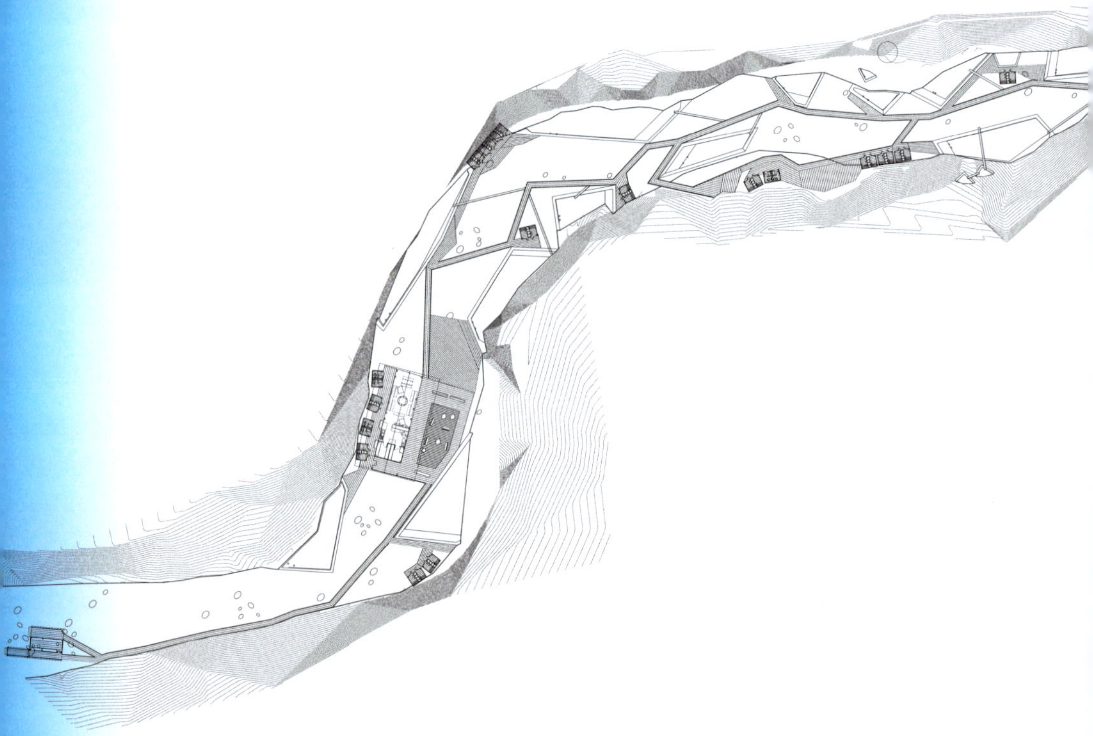

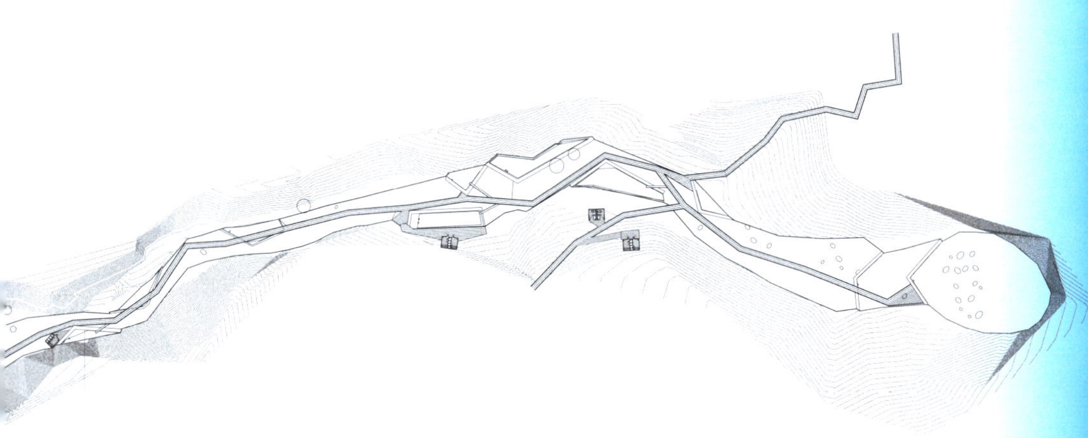

General plan

Las Tres Esperanzas

Towards an Architecture of Cooperation

In 2010, the exhibition *Small Scale, Big Change: New Architectures of Social Engagement* at the Museum of Modern Art in New York City surveyed eleven architectural projects scattered over five continents.[1] This exhibition consisting of architectures that foster new ways of inhabiting the built environment of neglected and peripheral communities was curated by Andrés Lepik. The design and construction processes shown were developed through collaboration between architects and the communities involved, both parties acknowledged to be articulators of a process of social, economic, and political transformation, working through small-scale projects.

Four years later, with a similar focus, the exhibition *The Architect Is Present* was organized at the Museo ICO in Madrid, curated by Luis Fernández-Galiano. This time, five international studios were represented, with works that sought to meet the needs of society and

1 The architects and firms represented in the exhibition were Diébédo Francis Kéré, from Burkina Faso; ELEMENTAL, from Chile; Noero Wolff Architects, from South Africa; Anna Heringer and Eike Roswag, from Germany; Hashim Sarkis A.L.U.D., from Lebanon; Urban-Think Tank, from Venezuela; Jorge Mario Jáuregui, from Brazil; Frédéric Druot, Anne Lacaton, and Jean Philippe Vassal, from France; and Michael Maltzan Architecture, Rural Studio, and Estudio Teddy Cruz, from the United States.

Al Borde
Puerto Cabuyal, Ecuador, 2009-2014

make the most of the scant resources available.[2] The exhibition focused on the value of inexpensive yet noble materials —clay, bamboo, wood, and ceramic— as part of an architecture that promotes a future based on local construction techniques. Both exhibitions illustrated themes of common interest to a group of contemporary architects and invited discussion about the social significance of architecture and a return to the artisanal values of the discipline.

Along similar lines, it is worth looking back to what the experience of Las Tres Esperanzas (The Three Hopes) has meant to Latin American architecture: constructive actions undertaken by Al Borde, revisited fifteen years after the execution of the first version of the school, perhaps in order to escape the enormous buzz the work created in the specialized media at the time and also to make room for the lucidity that comes with the passing of time.

Las Tres Esperanzas stands for creating architecture on the periphery. If, in first-world countries, the scale of works of this kind renders them of little interest to architecture firms, it is precisely this element that offers Al Borde a small opportunity for experimentation

2 The architects and studios included in the exhibition were Diébédo Francis Kéré, from Burkina Faso, TYIN tegnestue Architects, from Norway; Anupama Kundoo, from India; Solano Benítez, from Paraguay; and Anna Heringer, from Germany.

and inventiveness, motivated by the cultural context. This design has been configured on the basis of collective participation, and the result is a mestizo work, which defines its own architectural expression. The studio designed, constructed, and activated this small piece of rural infrastructure with what there was at hand, creating a contemporary architectural language out of the dialogue between preexisting elements and matter, whose rotund presence bears witness to the visceral state of a practice undergoing constant change.

Gottfried Semper has affirmed that the basic elements of architecture emerge as an intuitive response to the immediate needs felt by human beings in the face of manifestations of nature. The architectural elements of Las Tres Esperanzas are determined by the physical environment in which the work is set and they configure a point of gathering and safekeeping associated with a primitive condition. The archaic design logic and constructive process, executed with whatever is available in the context, is articulated by the climatic manifestations of the territory. As a consequence, functional architectural elements are constructed, whose language is based on the extension of the physical properties of matter, which aspires to be material.

The simple use of the natural materials of the local context is part of the transformation of this built environment, which gives shape to a striking architecture of fragile elements. By means of knots and moorings, a piece of wickerwork covered with thatch configures the structure in tectonic terms. In the creative process, the local vernacular has not been filtered through a romantic vision or in the aim of replicating ancient typologies. Certain architectural components are rather considered with the same ingenuity that is present in the anonymous constructions of the place.

The passage of time makes it possible to affirm that Las Tres Esperanzas goes beyond mere construction and contributes an experience about architecture, an architecture of cooperation, which incorporates traditional skills and knowledge among its most significant aspects. This architecture of humility has made Al Borde seem to be a group of "discalced" architects. That is a Latin American attitude, expressed through an architecture that does not conceal its own defects and whose surfaces bear witness to the passage of time and the wounds inherent in inhabiting the territory.

José Luis Uribe

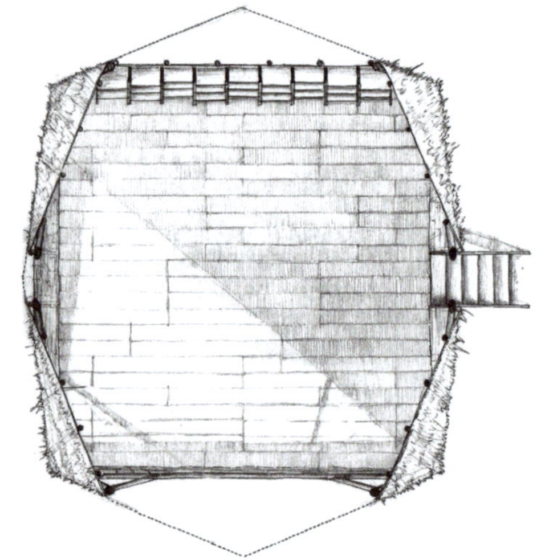

Nueva Esperanza School. Plan

Nueva Esperanza School. West elevation

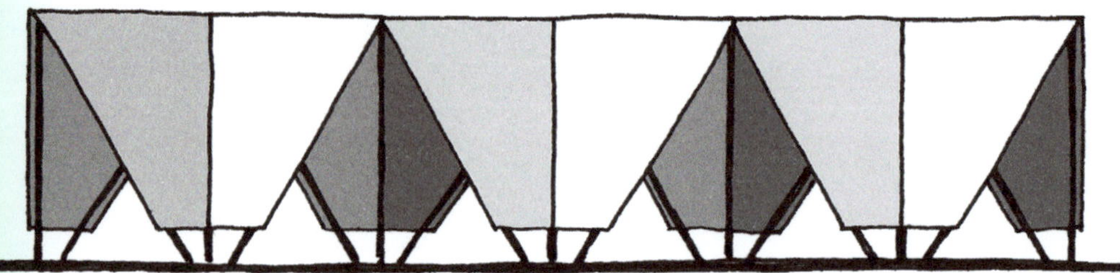

Esperanza Dos. Elevation

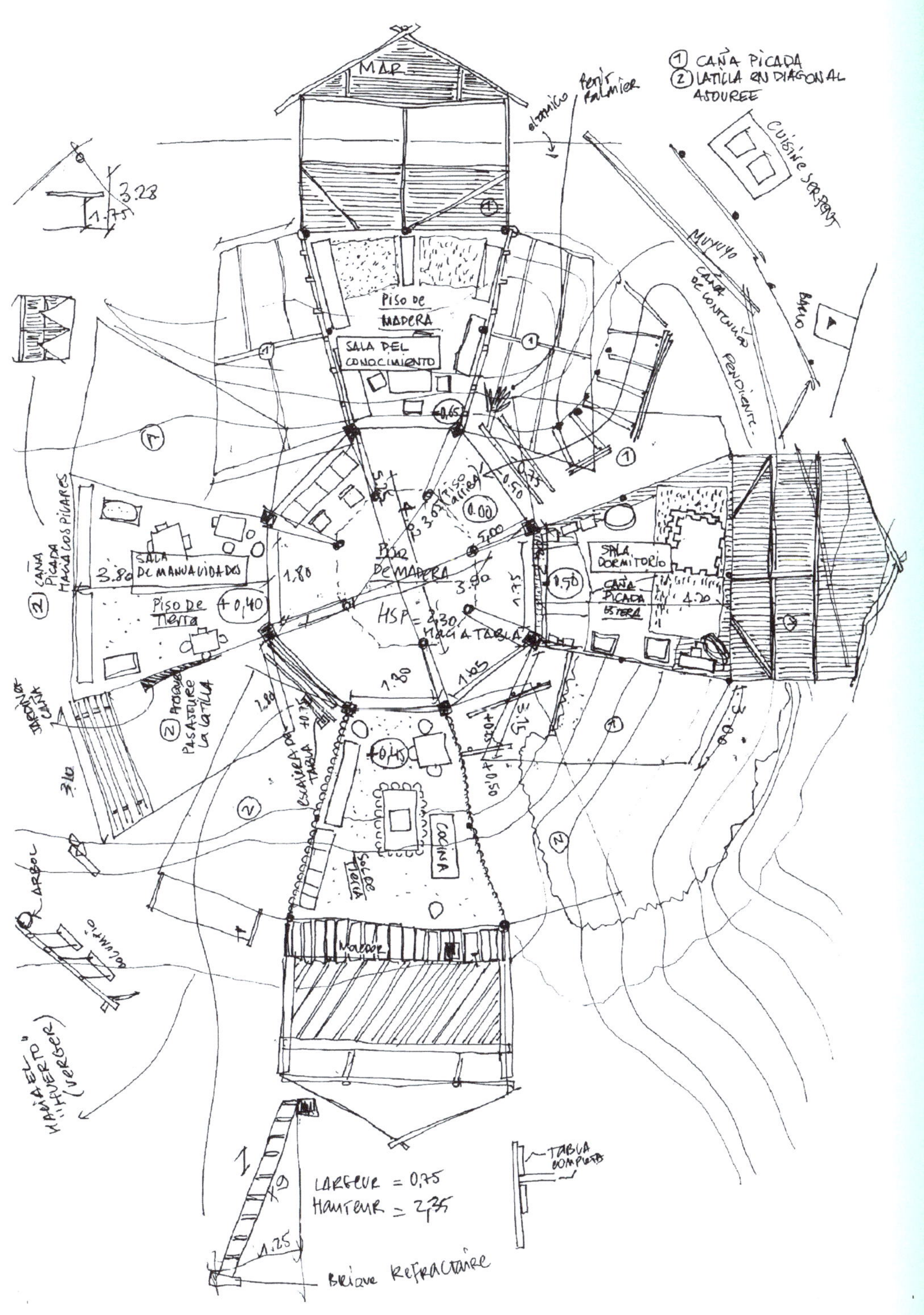
MAR
1 CAÑA PICADA
2 LATILLA EN DIAGONAL
ASOUREE
CUISINE SERPENT
PISO DE MADERA
SALA DEL CONOCIMIENTO
SALA DE MANUALIDADES
PISO DE TIERRA
SALA DORMITORIO
CAÑA PICADA
ARBOL
COCINA
LARGEUR = 0,75
HAUTEUR = 2,35
TABLA COMPLETA
BRIQUE REFRACTAIRE

LENGUAJE
Trabajos
Terminados
JUEGOS y LEGOS
Libretas

Teletón Children's Rehabilitation Center

> I believe in clashes in my mouth... I like to eat something delicious with a wine that contrasts with it, and for both to fight to convince me which is best.
>
> —Francis Mallman

I should start by saying that any reading of mine of the work of Solano Benítez's studio Gabinete de Arquitectura will necessarily be shaped by the couple of conversations I had many moons ago with Rafael Iglesias, an architect from my hometown of Rosario, Argentina. We are fortunate to live in an age that is comfortable with concepts that seem contradictory but which, by being accepted, produce the excitement of new coherences.

The Teletón Children's Rehabilitation Center is the building I am writing about, but I suspect that what I have to say applies to most of Benítez's work. One could wield the argument that the best state for architecture is one of incompletion. Perhaps that is why we are fascinated by works under construction. This building possesses the power of transmitting that quality of not being finished, and that is what makes it extraordinary: it invites us to imagine multiple realities, to continue a dialogue, and it makes visitors feel that they are part of a continuity in a state of permanent transformation.

Another idea it inspires is that of the collapse of time, essential in the quest for the incomplete. The use of familiar materials that nevertheless behave in an unusual way makes us scratch our heads: "I know exactly what that is, but somehow if displaces me from the ordinary to the sublime." We can neither quantify it nor give a completely rational account of it: something that should be, if not an obligation, at least an aspiration of any work of architecture worthy of the name. Let us make one thing clear: this building is real. It is not a speculation, but its poetical form seems to render real an ideal of beauty. The ability to reconcile tradition with innovation reinvigorates qualities that define its essence of belonging to local cultures, but also connects us with our humanity, which is more universal that we are generally willing to say aloud. Architecture is a universal language, humanistic to the core. The goal of the projects of Gabinete de Arquitectura is part of that humanism, which is necessarily incomplete, ambiguous, and imperfect.

Nothing is more complex that what is familiar to us; nothing is more literal than everyday things. In this sense, the architecture of Solano

Benítez is marvelously poetic, as it modifies what is familiar and transforms it into something much more sophisticated.

The clashes referred to in the quotation from Francis Mallman need not be resolved: on the contrary, the fight has to continue, without either of the tastes or feelings managing to convince. Tension must be maintained at all costs. The Teletón Children's Rehabilitation Center succeeds in maintaining that ambiguity as a way of honoring the human condition. What more can be demanded of a piece of architecture?

Hernán Díaz Alonso

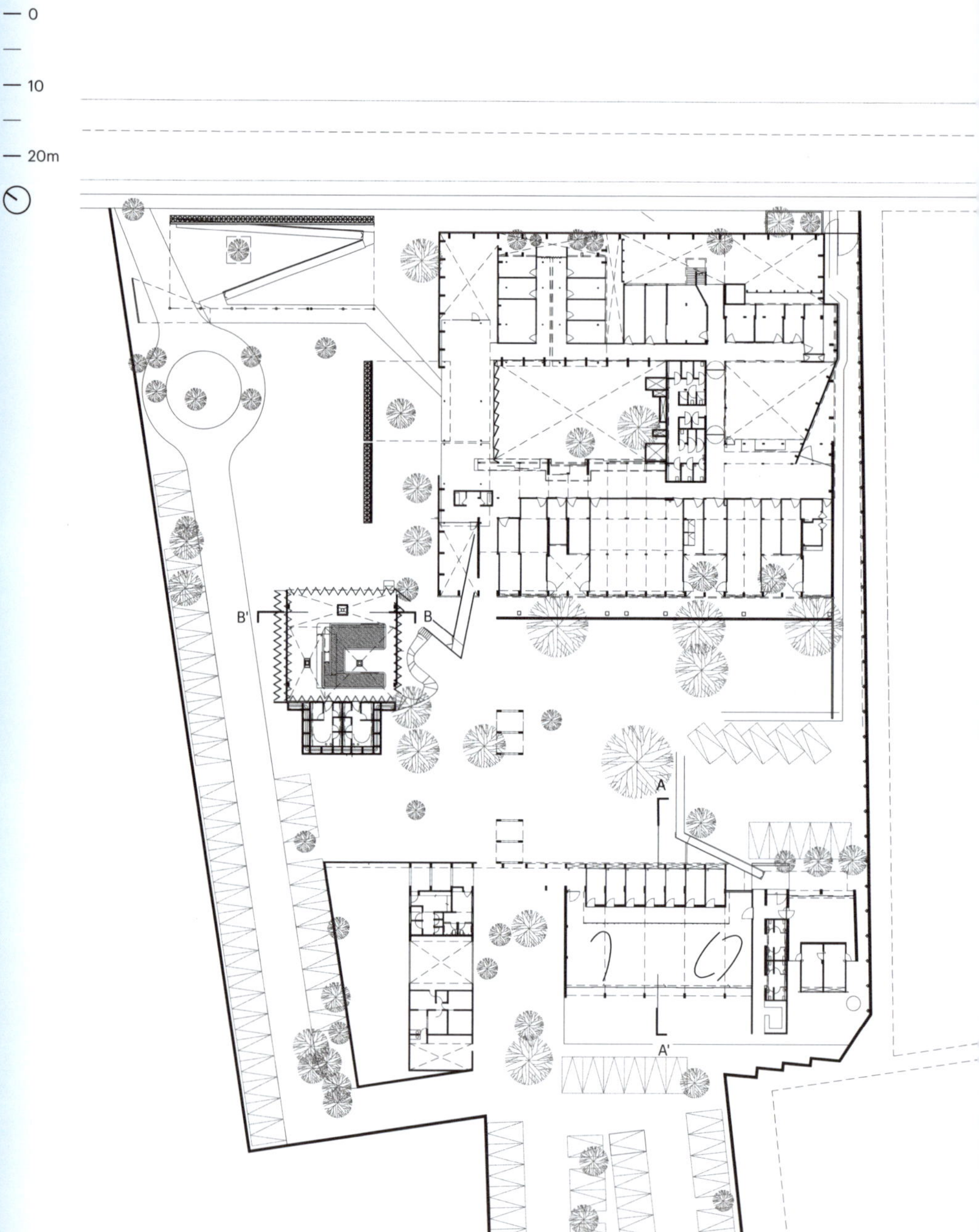

0

10

20m

B'
B
A
A'

Plan

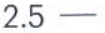

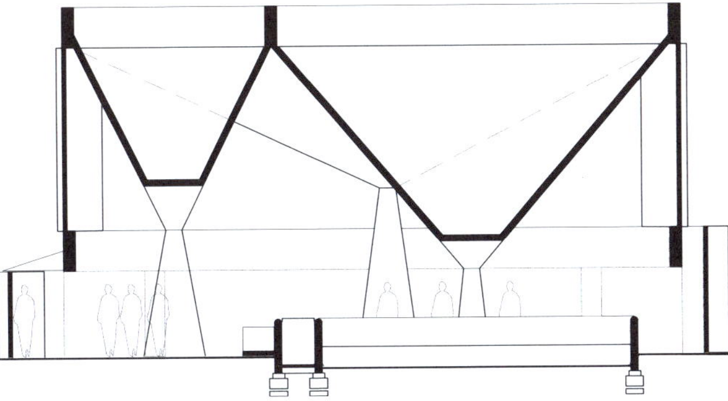

Section A-A'

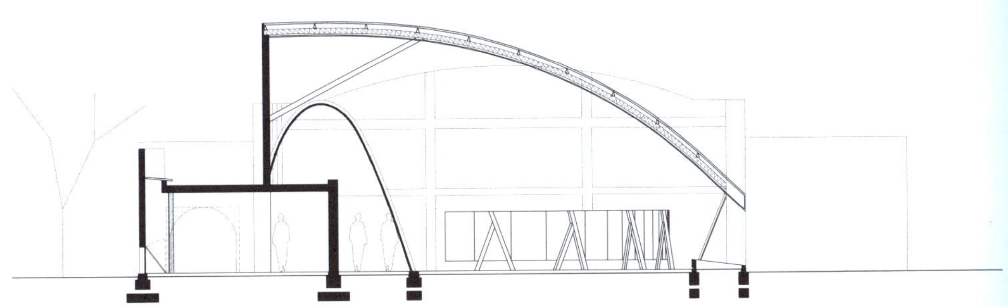

Section B-B'

Bienvenidos

Parque Cultural Valparaíso

In April 1999, the 1,300 inmates of the Valparaíso Public Prison were transferred to a new penitentiary on the outskirts of the city. The process was masterfully recorded in the documentary *Arcana* (2006) by architect and filmmaker Cristóbal Vicente, who filmed the interior of the prison during its last year of existence. In the final sequence of *Arcana*, the camera rises from the prison's central courtyard to offer a view of the city and port of Valparaíso from the air. This image shows the privileged geographical situation of the prison: a flat stretch of tableland on the summit of a hill surrounded by the urban conglomeration, with a 360-degree panorama, from the geographical amphitheater of the bay to the Pacific Ocean: a view that the inmates were never able to appreciate.

When it was decided to vacate the prison, which had been in use since 1843, it was also understood that the site would necessarily be important to the city. Shortly after it was vacated, groups of local artists occupied the space in an organic manner, transforming it into a self-governing cultural center. It was thanks to them, not only that the site did not fall into the claws of the real estate market, but also that it was given a civic and cultural character.

This vocation was revalidated in 2007, when Oscar Niemeyer donated the draft project of a cultural center for the site. The proposal,

HLPS Arquitectos
Valparaíso, Chile, 2011

similar to his design for the Centro Cultural Internacional in Ávila, Spain, was approved by the administration of the time. Images leaked to the media, however, provoked resistance from local communities to the project by the Brazilian architect, because it did away with the preexisting constructions on the site. Niemeyer refused to modify his proposal.

Since the transformation of the former prison into a cultural center had been announced in 2009, the government was obliged to hold a competition for the design of the new Parque Cultural de Valparaíso (PCV). With a proposal that respected the preexisting structures, maximized the public use of the plateau, and creatively exploited the topography of the site, the competition was won by the young architects of HLPS: Jonathan Holmes, Martín Labbé, Carlonia Portugueis, and Osvaldo Spichiger.

Opened to the public in 2012, the complex designed by HLPS consists of two L-shaped volumes, one of them preexisting, which flank a flat green area with views over the bay. In spite of their solid appearance, the volumes are not closed. The former cellblock has been expanded to the exterior wall of the prison and its first level opens up toward the east, while the three interior levels are illuminated by natural light from above. Some of the graffiti and wall paintings left by the inmates can still be seen on the walls. The new building opens up in stages toward the north, with a large shaded balcony looking seaward. Built of exposed concrete, with an air of public infrastructure that recalls the school of architecture and urbanism of the Universidade de São Paulo, by João Vilanova Artigas (1969), this volume, thanks to its sober elegance, has become the new image of the PCV.

Quite apart from the meticulous design, the PCV is important because it opened up possibilities that had seemed unfeasible before, at least in Chile: first of all, the fact that organized communities were able to sunder an alliance between municipal authorities and *starchitects* that seemed indestructible in the early years of this century; secondly, that a team of young architects were able successfully to carry out a project of this scope and quality. Moreover, the outcome destroyed the myth that the government was necessarily a bad client that would ruin any architect's design. And finally, the PCV demonstrated that care for local heritage does not prevent good projects from being executed, especially in a city like Valparaíso, which had just shortly before been classified as a World Heritage Site.

The conditions that made possible the PCV deserve to be considered as the necessary guarantors of the success of any public project: engaged and organized citizens, capable of administering a space and demanding that the authorities make public use of it; a serious and responsible state apparatus, which realizes that its role is not to impose visions on society but rather to gather together those that already exist and channel them through professional management, with teams of committed technicians; an urban renovation project that starts out with respect for the site; an architectural design that maximizes the supply of public space; and a model of cultural administration that can sustain these spaces over time and ensure their public viability, the maintenance of the installations, and the quality of the cultural products they offer. Of course not all of these conditions fall within the realm of architecture per se: that is precisely the difficulty. In the end, good buildings are collective initiatives in which we architects play only a partial role. However well we do our own work, if others things do not function, our projects will be condemned to failure.

The PCV is an example of how cities can be built by an alliance of wills that does not require stars of the discipline to put them on the map. Which does not mean, of course, that the intervention of the architects is irrelevant.

As we saw in *Arcana*, the only way to escape from the former prison was by air, like Icarus. Today, with its complete visual dominance over the surroundings, the PCV is not a place from which we would wish to escape. We can even observe the walls of the former prison without anxiety, without even realizing that they were once used to confine. We are in a space of reclusion that has been transformed into one of openness. In the face of a project like the PCV, the real question is whether the prisons we continue to construct today will ever be reconverted into buildings and public spaces as powerful as this one.

Francisco Díaz

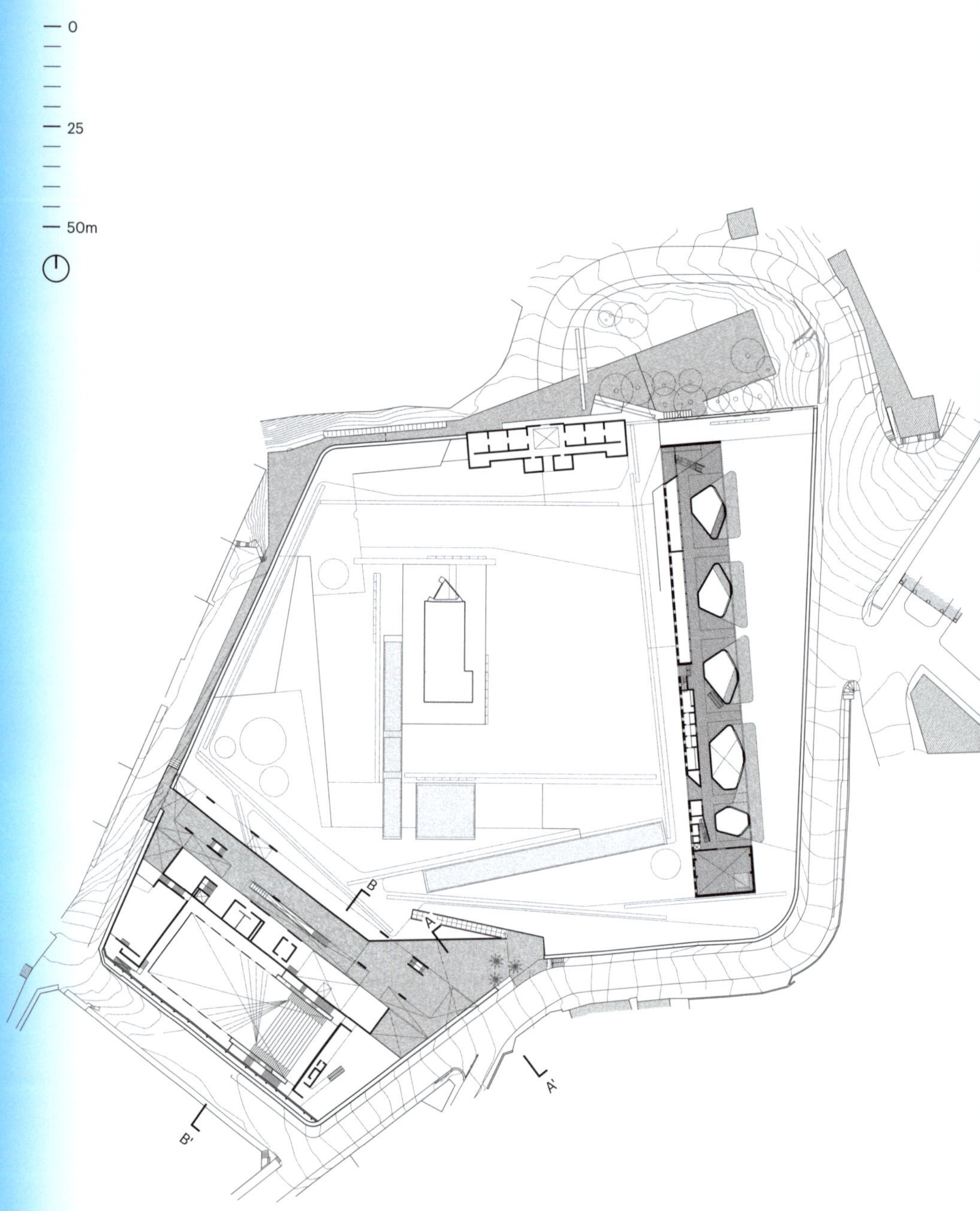

Plan

0 —

5 —

10m —

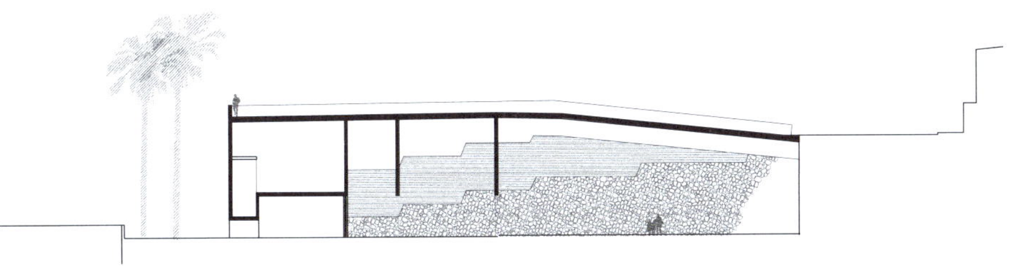

Section A-A'

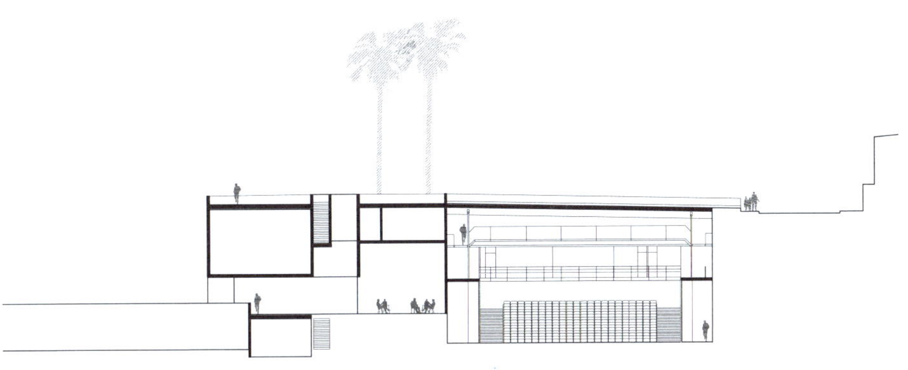

Section B-B'

La Tallera Siqueiros

La Tallera, so named by David Alfaro Siqueiros "in homage to Woman, the creator of life" (*tallera* is a "feminized" form of the masculine noun *taller* ['workshop'] in Spanish) was conceived in 1965 as a studio where the artist could work on the large-format murals commissioned by the Hotel de la Selva, which would later occupy what is now known as the Polyforum Siqueiros, in the Hotel de México.[1] Siqueiros called it the world's first workshop for muralists, although its physical characteristics and machinery made it look more like a mechanic's garage. Nevertheless, it was soon to become a multidisciplinary space for artistic creation and served as the muralist's studio house during his final years.

The site itself and the murals that remained there later suffered years of neglect and abandonment, which left them almost in ruins. In 2010, the Consejo Nacional para la Cultura y las Artes, a now-defunct federal cultural agency, organized a public competition for their restoration and the establishment of a new cultural epicenter. Frida Escobedo proposed three clear and specific actions: the creation of a public plaza as an antechamber to the murals; turning the murals that flanked the workshop patio toward the city and

1 "Historia La Tallera," Instituto Nacional de Bellas Artes y Literatura, Secretaría de Cultura: https://saps-latallera.org/tallera/historia.

opening up the original workshop space toward the plaza; and establishing a semitransparent filter so that the more domestic interior spaces could be subtly but firmly connected to the more productive exterior spaces. These daring gestures are also political actions. Siqueiros was a radical revolutionary and everything he did was political. Frida's intervention was also political, and she understood the politics by which it was executed.

The building invests all of its spatial and economic capital on these three strategies, knowing that public and cultural works in Mexico inevitably suffer from budgetary shortages, whether funds are needed to activate them or to maintain them.

Pier Vittorio Aureli has analyzed "the city's form as an act —or project— that defines a political intentionality, thus establishing a precondition for engagement with the city's complex nature." In the preface to *The City as Project*, the city is defined "not as a mere mass of flows and programs but as a political form."[2] The murals are here transformed into *citizens* surrounded by a plaza, which becomes a place belonging to all. It is the plaza that negotiates with the cultural authorities of the government in turn, remaining

2 Pier Vittorio Aureli, *The City as a Project* (Berlin: Ruby Press, 2020), p. 10.

because the mural are and have been —now and always— citizens, and they determine the form of the city.

Public architecture in Mexico faces great challenges. Budgets are limited and time restraints strict, and the pressure of political interests generally results in works of scant architectural quality. Ensuring that the works continue to function as they should, as the years go by, is a further test. Frida Escobedo has faced both of these challenges with one audacious gesture.

Over the last ten years, as the architect predicted, the use of the interior space has depended on successive administrations. The plaza, however, will never lose its character, because it depends only on the murals, which rise up with stoicism to the call of their creator.

I don't know whether La Tallera will continue living up to the reasons for which Siqueiros gave it that name, but I am sure it will live up to Frida Escobedo's reasons and so remain a life-creating space.

Tatiana Bilbao

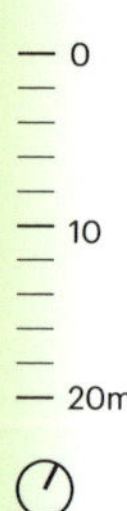

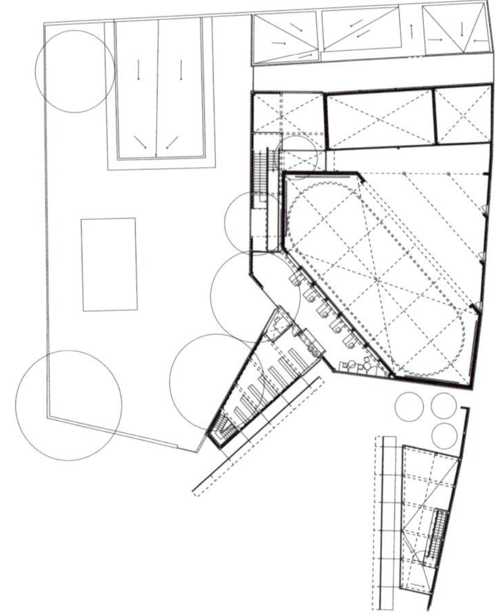

Upper floor plan

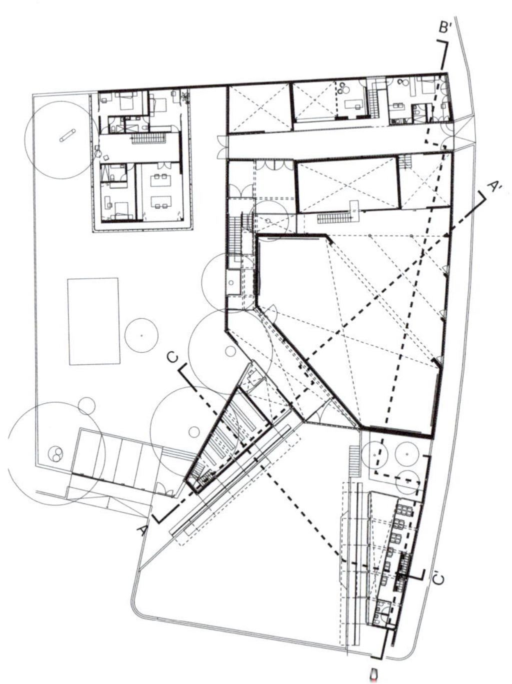

Ground floor plan

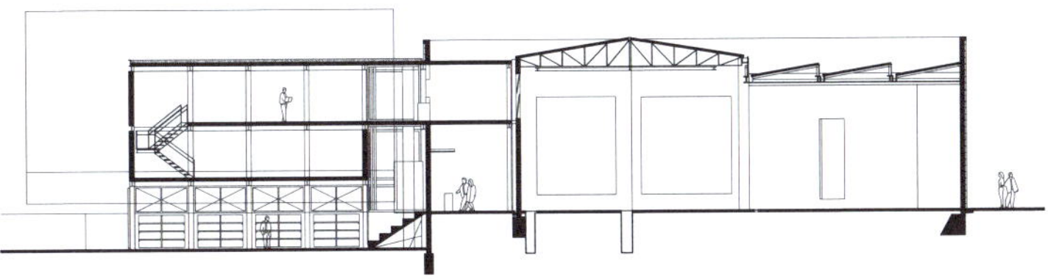

Section A-A'

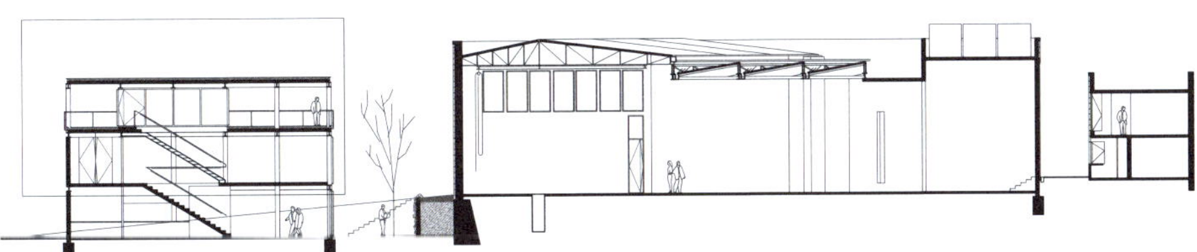

Section B-B'

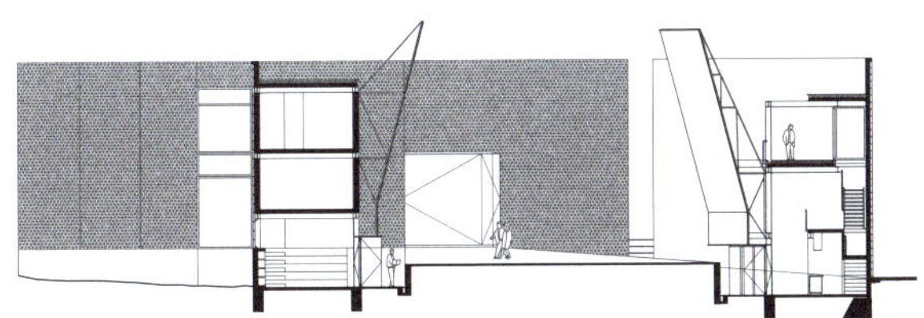

Section C-C'

Jardín Botánico Culiacán

[...] let's accept the role of gardener as being equal in dignity to the role of architect...
—Brian Eno

Arthur William Hill, the son of Daniel Hill, born in Watford, England in 1875, retired from business toward the end of the nineteenth century and devoted himself to the care of his garden, one of his principal interests. Since his childhood, Arthur had acquired great practical skill in various branches of horticulture. This determined his vocation, and in 1904 he became professor of botany at King's College, Cambridge, after having led an expedition to Bolivia and Peru in 1903. In 1907 he was appointed assistant director of the Royal Botanic Gardens at Kew. In 1915 Hill published a volume entitled *The History and Functions of Botanic Gardens*, which begins with this marvelous paragraph: "There are three things which have stimulated men throughout the ages to travel far and wide over the surface of the globe: gold, spices and drugs. It is to the two latter of these universal needs of man that we may trace the origin and foundation of botanic gardens."

At one of the talks organized by Hans Ulrich Obrist in the Garden Marathon series of the Serpentine Gallery (designed by Peter

Zumthor in 2011), artist, composer, and producer Brian Eno explained his understanding of how a musical composition was created by the difference between an architect and a gardener: "An architect, at least in the traditional sense, is somebody who has an in-detail concept of the final result in their head, and their task is to control the rest of nature sufficiently to get that built." Everything, he added, is "subject to an effort of control." A gardener, on the other hand, works "in collaboration with the complex and unpredictable processes of nature." That is what gardens are like. They are not created, not controlled down to every last detail —not even the Garden of Eden—: they are cultivated. One chooses the best seeds one can find and hopes they will do their thing, trusting that the result will be reasonably successful.

Carlos Murillo, an engineer by training and an architect (and then a designer of gardens) by vocation, was born in Culiacán, Sinaloa, in 1925. He studied at the Universidad de Guadalajara, graduating in 1948. He chose engineering for the same reason as Luis Barragán, another well-known graduate of the school, who would also embrace garden design as a vocation: at that time there was no architecture program at the university. Back in Culiacán in the early 1950s, Murillo constructed his first work: a house for Francisco Ritz. It was a clear example of the influence of the international style in

Mexico: free-standing walls, large windows, flat roof. The house included a patio with a garden.

Indeed, gardens became Murillo's passion, as well as his profession. He continued to design houses and gardens until in 1986 he convinced the governor of Sinaloa at the time to cede him some land adjacent to the university so that he could establish the Jardín Botánico Culiacán. Little by little Murillo transformed this area into both a garden and a didactic space. In the 1990s, Agustín Coppel, a local businessman, commissioned Murillo to design the gardens for a residential area he was developing. The professional relationship led to the amalgamation of Murillo's collection of plants and part of the art collection of Isabel and Agustín Coppel. Today, in addition to more than one thousand plant species, the botanical gardens contain works by contemporary artists, initially under the curatorship of Patrick Charpenel.

As befits a garden, the Jardín Botánico Culiacán has continued to grow and change over time, reflecting a fundamental aspect of Murillo's philosophy of landscape, as Coppel tells it. In order to organize the space and provide the necessary support service infrastructure for both the collection of plants and the artworks, Tatiana Bilbao's architecture firm was invited to collaborate. Following the death of Carlos Murillo, Bilbao worked with Taller de Operaciones Ambientales, a firm specializing in public architecture, on the design and organization of the landscape.

Bilbao's first task was to organize the botanical garden by means of paths that would define zones, and then to try out various methods of laying out these paths. She opted for one that justifies the absence of method, or rather for an abstract one, which works at a distance, from the air. The paths of a garden that is ready to go, that is literally "in progress," are laid out by walking it: the constant search for open ground and the best shortcuts organize the space of the garden. Thus, the strategy was to superpose the blurred image of the branches of any tree in the garden onto the plan of the site and then to reconcile the resulting layout with the existing circumstances.

The paths generated different zones. To accompany the plant species, works by artists such as Dan Graham, Richard Long, Teresa Margolles, Tercerunquinto, Francis Alÿs, and Olafur Eliasson, as well as many others, were installed. Some of the services were also inserted amidst the paths: educational modules and a small open auditorium. Constructed of exposed concrete, these monolithic volumes avoid orthogonal forms without striving after the effects of distortion. Bright, friendly bunkers, they are forms and structures that do not seek to blend into the surrounding greenery by either their compositional strategies or their exterior materials, but neither do they pursue contrast for its own sake.

The design of the spaces required time, just as cultivating a garden does. During the process, the team at Bilbao's studio rethought their strategies and considered variations on public buildings conceived not as enormous rocks, which avoid right angles, but rather as simple, almost iconic forms, which Bilbao defined as described geometries. Thus, the project developed rather like the garden in which it was inserted, as a work in progress, open-ended, clear in its aims, but variable in its details: a work in which architecture seeks to learn from an engineer turned gardener.

Alejandro Hernández Gálvez

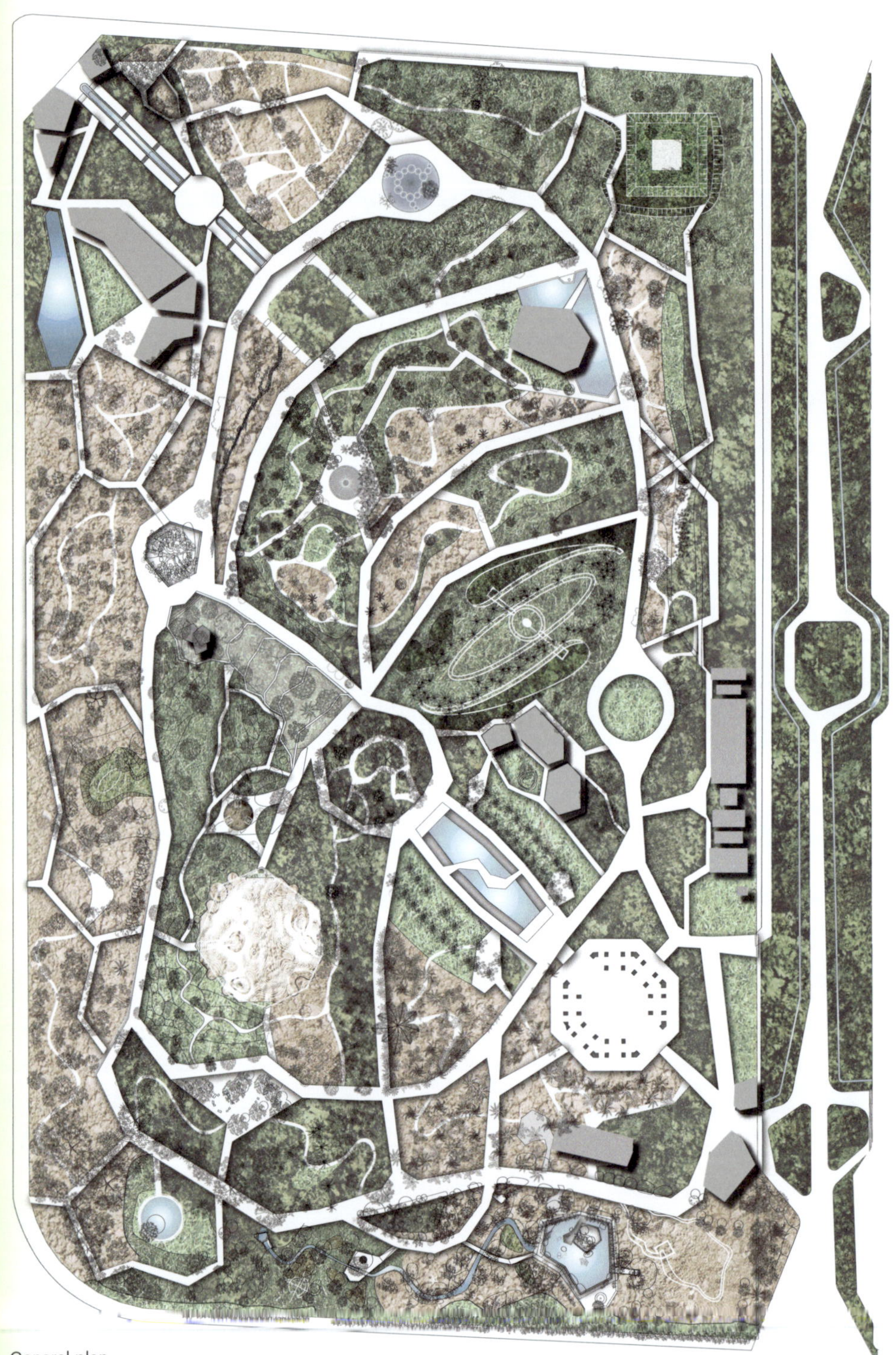

General plan

0
2.5
5m

Section A-A'

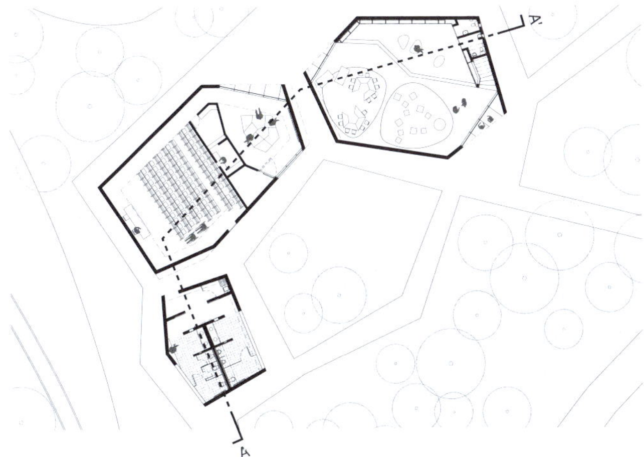

Auditorium floor plan

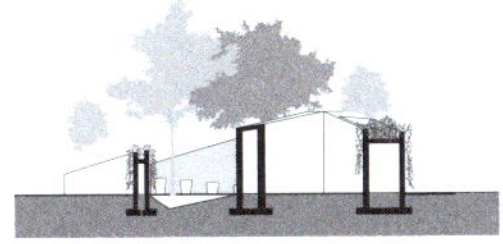

Section B-B'

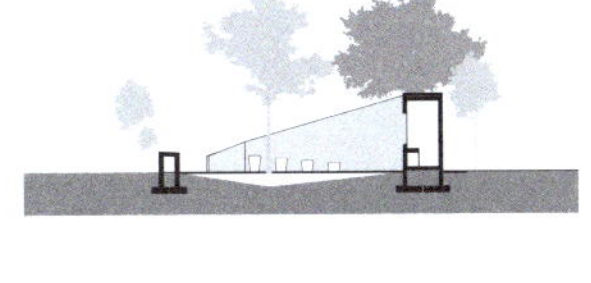

Section C-C'

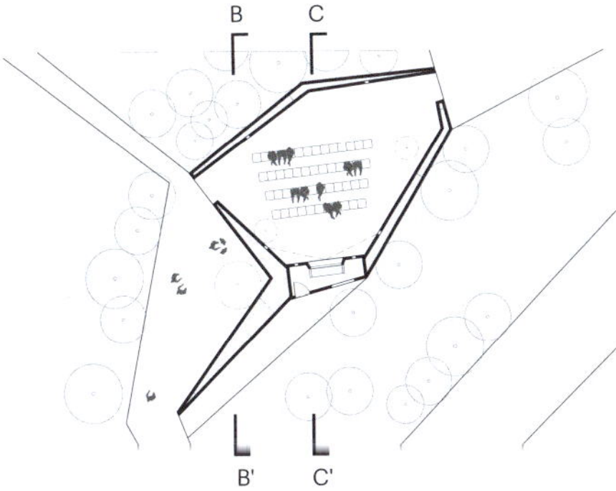

Open auditorium floor plan

Centro Cultural San Pablo

The sense of predictability is always comforting when one navigates a colonial town such as Oaxaca, laid out in accordance with the Laws of the Indies on a grid pattern, with north-south and east-west orientation. Within this strict logic, the discovery of a place hidden in the center of block is always a moment of great astonishment and emotion.

After centuries of transformations, adaptations, expansions, and additions, the creation of the Centro Cultural San Pablo, which includes the former monastery of Santo Domingo de Soriano and the chapel dedicated to Our Lady of the Rosary, has been the result of a painstaking and laborious archeological operation. The Taller de Arquitectura Mauricio Rocha + Gabriela Carrillo opted for the elimination of all the later post-colonial structures, so that the oldest buildings could come into their own. Once this operation had been completed, there were insufficient areas to meet the requirements of the program, so new architectural spaces were constructed.

The new elements exhibit both materials and a constructive language totally different from those of the preexisting structure, built in stone, but they do maintain its floor-to-ceiling dimensions, its horizontal rhythms (derived from the original fenestration), and its straight lines. Made of wood, steel, and glass, these new elements are arranged around the central courtyard to house the main offices of the Fundación Alfred Harp Helú Oaxaca and a restaurant recently transformed into an art gallery. A third component operates as an insertion into the central courtyard area of the former monastery to fill out the library spaces.

The arrangement makes for some marvelous spatial details, such as the long, narrow patio that opens to the left of the entrance to the monastery, with its curious façade of openings in which what seem to be offerings and devotional objects have been placed. This axis terminates in a leafy tree that rises up as the true protagonist of the space. The juxtapositions of new and old are near in proximity, but respectful of each other: they approach, but they do not touch. The added elements are self-supporting and neither alter nor depend on the original structure.

In the buildings around the exterior courtyard, the slender double wooden columns are joined by steel beams, which are connected in turn to wooden joists by means of a perpendicular panel inserted into the section. In the case of the new element inserted into the courtyard of the monastery, the double columns are of steel and support a glass façade that completes one side of the central space. The contrast with the thick stone pillars and arcades is accentuated.

Exposure to the elements in the patio is attenuated by movable translucent panels that determine the angle of the light filtering into the interior, while slight separations in the new stone paving, as though there were sliding flagstones, provide for the runoff of rainwater. A small, simple pool, placed at an angle, reflects the structure surrounding it. There are numerous other details that express the delicate ongoing dialogue between old and new: the grooved wooden door handles, the steps incorporated into the capital of a column, the indirect lighting suspended from the beams, and the contemporary art objects, such as the entrance grille, designed by Francisco Toledo.

In spite of my fascination with these details, what I most admire about the Centro Cultural San Pablo is the way the public spaces are accessed by visitors. The astonishment mentioned above is provoked by the deep vista that opens up into the city block. This is a long passageway that crosses the block —from Avenida de la Independencia to Avenida Miguel Hidalgo—, characterized by a compact composition of materials and elements: a pavement of long, narrow bricks laid down in a fishbone design, surrounded by thick grass, a wall partly covered by cactus vines, two trees that provide shade, and raised platforms with a stone edge on which visitors can sit and enjoy the space. I have often sat on this edge to watch what was going on around me: people walking by, couples conversing, people sitting in the café, or coming in or out of the chapel, the cultural center, or the library.

The Centro Cultural San Pablo is one of those spaces in which time seems to go by more slowly. The simplicity of the simple, geometrical gestures is complemented by the richness of the materials, the pleasant microclimate, and the opportunity to share with others on a scale that is at once private, inclusive, and plural. Every time I visit Oaxaca I return to this place. Even if I have just a few minutes, I choose to use them to pass through this singular urban landscape. Although the center is private property, and there is a security guard who can deny access, the Centro Cultural San Pablo functions as a place that welcomes those who have discovered it and who somehow appreciate this kind of experience in the city.

Demand for public space will always exceed the available supply, especially in cities and towns whose populations continue to grow. The trend of capitalist growth is toward the privatization of spaces. Without being familiar with the details of the different premises and design decisions that configured the landscape of the Centro Cultural San Pablo, I can nevertheless affirm that the achievement of having created conditions in which people can not only use and take advantage of public equipment, but also enjoy a space not intended for profit or consumption —simply an open public space— is perhaps the aspect of this project that I most admire, and I applaud the aims and efforts of the architects.

Elisa Silva

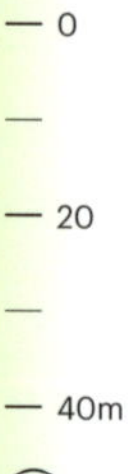

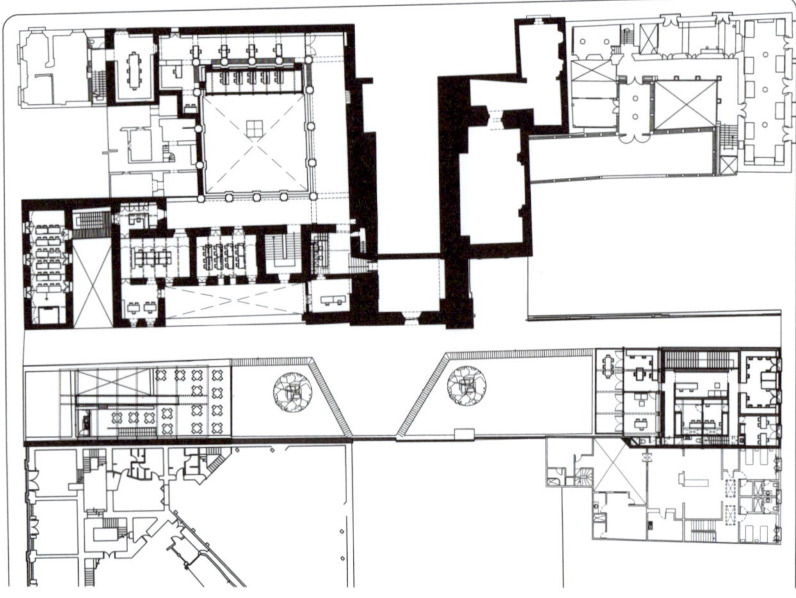

Level 1

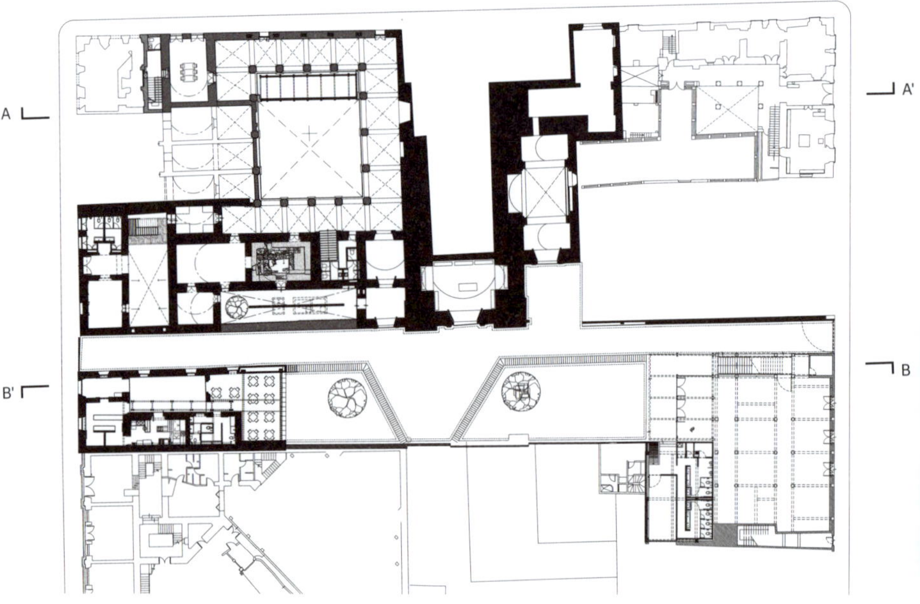

Ground floor plan

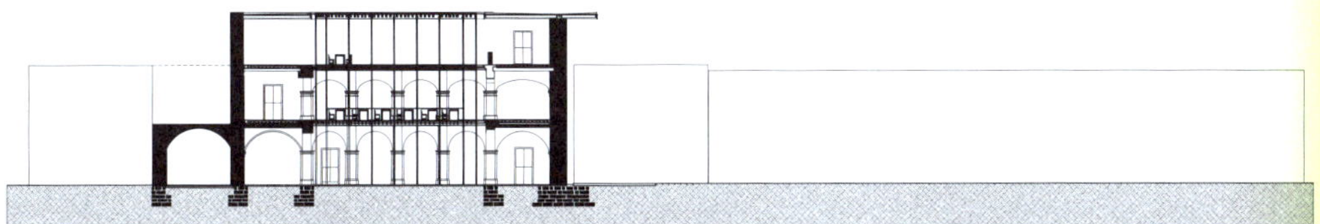

Section A-A'

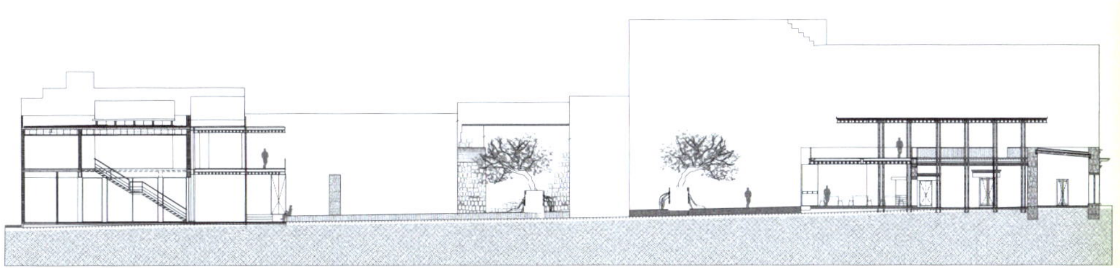

Section B-B'

Museo Jumex

David Chipperfield's museums are often characterized by what we might call a sculptural neoclassicism: an extended composition of rectangular boxes united by a modular, rhythmical language on their façades. The Museo Jumex, however, belongs to a different family. Located on a narrow lot, squeezed in between shopping centers, office towers, the Teatro Cervantes, and the Museo Soumaya, the building shows itself to be a robust and compact volume. A significant detail —the gradual widening of the travertine cladding of the façade— underlines how mass and solidity increase toward the upper part. The building recalls certain brutalist structures which, like inverted pyramids, balance monolithic bodies on smaller bases. Owing to the solidity of its materials, it is a volume that, in the architect's own formulation, brings to mind a pre-Hispanic sculpture.

At first glance, the building's elegant silhouette seems to reflect the traditional typology of the saw-tooth roof, which serves to provide the exhibition rooms with diffuse northerly light, but a second look calls into question this obvious conclusion. The openings are located in the slanted part of the roof, oriented toward the southwest, offering a hint of the formal and sculptural aspirations that have come into play in defining their arrangement. The building strikes a singular pose within the urban context —not unlike the Museo

Soumaya in this respect—, resembling a piece of furniture, a sort of outsized chest of drawers. The thick columns on the ground floor, the openings on the intermediate level, and the rockabilly hairdo of the serrated roof lend an anthropomorphic character to the building: an astonishing Hejdukian animal strolling through a linear park.

Apart from this striking figure, what distinguishes the Museo Jumex in terms of the challenges facing the discipline? In the end, what matters is not so much what can be written about the building itself, but rather what it tells us about other museums. How does this building question the typology of the contemporary art museum?

I remember having attended a talk Chipperfield gave at the Universidad Iberoamericana when he was designing the Museo Jumex. The English architect showed a variety of arrangements he had considered for the triangular lot. The only constant was the need to make visible the interior —the art— from the public space, and vice versa, that is, to make the urban surroundings visible from the exhibition rooms. The real problem of the typology of the contemporary art museum, explained Chipperfield, is that it resists openness, transparency, and permeability. Owing precisely to its function as a container of pieces of art, it demands enclosed spaces, protected from the exterior. The neighboring institution illustrates this to perfection: the Museo Soumaya is a great blind volume that encloses its interior spaces. World's fair architecture.

When architects seek the opposite, when they try to create a certain openness and permeability, they generally achieve no more than a glass-paned entrance lobby. The rhetoric of transparency and the democratization formulated in the mission statements of art institutions is at loggerheads with the conservation requirements of the collections, with those who lend the works, and with the insurance companies involved. It would appear to be an insoluble puzzle. More than once, the result has been a timid display window overlooking the sidewalk, which is soon filled with ticket windows, a coatroom, a gift shop, a café, etc. Instead of rendering the art visible, the museum itself is promoted as a consumer space: a high culture mini-mall. A perfect example of the problem expounded by Chipperfield is the New Museum by SANAA in New York City. But how to link what is going on within an art institution with the context that surrounds it?

In responding to this question, Chipperfield proposed creating an intermediate floor, a loggia that not only offers visitors an elevated view of the immediate context, but also constitutes a totally transparent floor: a glazed rectangle, surrounded by open galleries.

Inadequate for presenting art in its more traditional formats (there are no walls or sufficient protection from sunlight), the floor is used for installations, performances, lectures, debates, informal talks, and the projection of films. This flexible space can be darkened by means of a large curtain around the perimeter in order to compensate the lack of an auditorium space, given the limited size of the project. This intermediate floor is complemented by an open gallery, its height carefully gaged, that seeks a separation from the surrounding space without completely isolating itself: an open-air *piano nobile*. It is a space at once intimate and exposed, which houses specific elements, such as the museum's large open lobby. Before gaining access to the air-conditioned spaces, one enters the museum from beneath a two-sided gable that emphasizes the transition from the exterior world of travertine (the mineral nature of the metropolis) to the interior world of white concrete (an anticipation of the plaster environment of the exhibition rooms). Both spaces seek to mitigate the museum's condition as a blank container, transforming it into a magical box with links between within and without. It is an ambitious endeavor which, behind its classic materials and the use of traditional architectural tools, faces up to the typological crisis, demands that exhibition formats be reconsidered, and inspires public responsibility for a museum in the city.

Wonne Ickx

0
5
10m

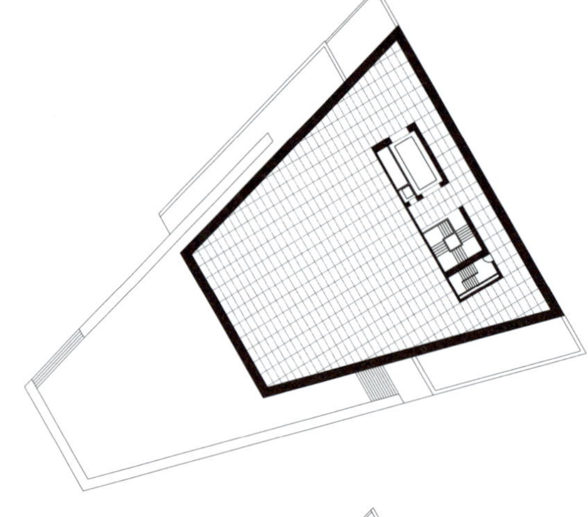

Level 2

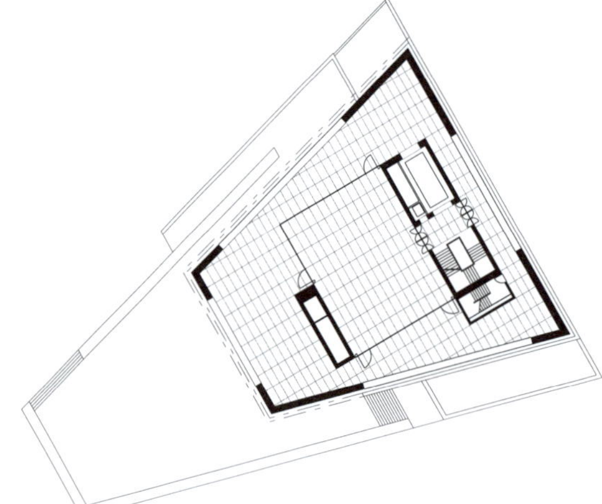

Level 1

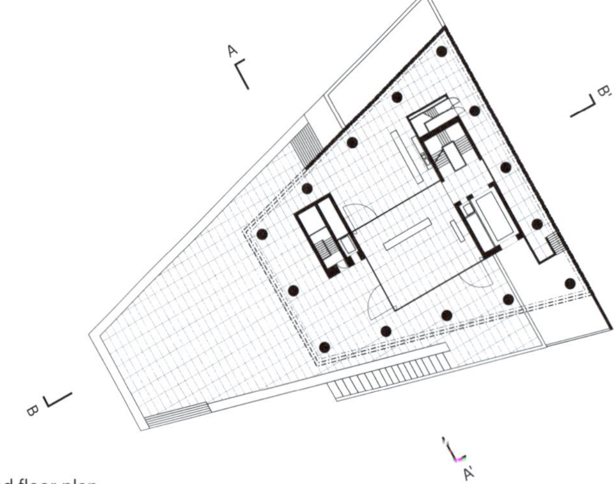

Ground floor plan

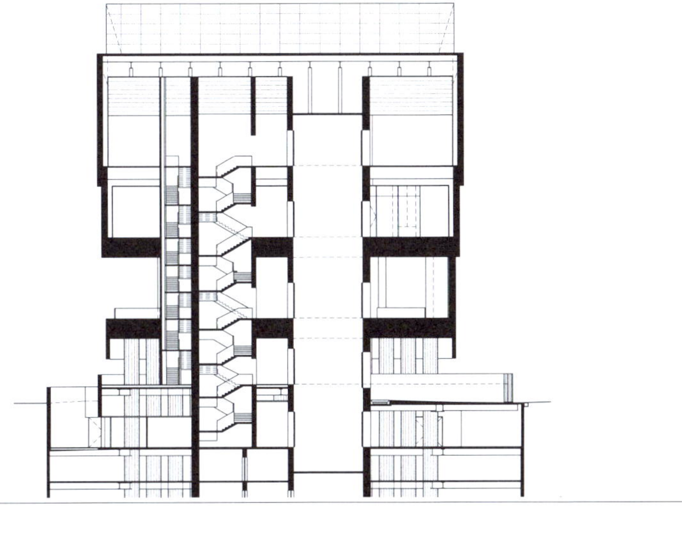

Section A-A'

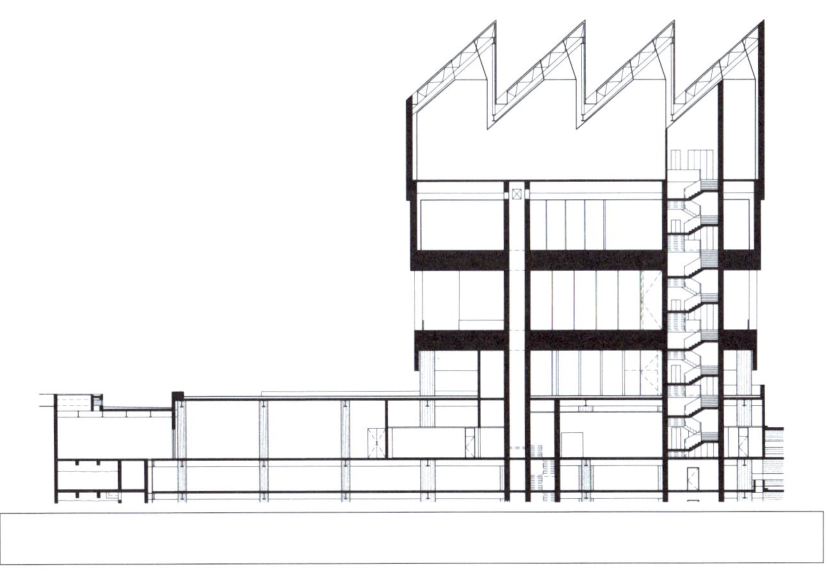

Section B-B'

infinitum
COSTCO

telcel

MUSEO JUMEX

MUSEO JUMEX

MUSEO JUMEX

Lugar de la Memoria

¡Ceded al nuevo impar
potente de orfandad!

[Give way to the new odd number
mighty with orphanhood!]

César Vallejo, "XXXVI", *Trilce.*

Lugar de la Memoria [The Place of Remembrance], Barclay & Crousse's indelible work of architecture, is a place for healing as much as it is for remembrance, an austere structure for reflection and reconciliation in the aftermath of two of the most destructive and violent decades of recent Peruvian history. Conflict, perpetuated both by terrorism (the Shining Path guerilla movement) and a socioeconomic crisis, resulted in the deaths of more than sixty thousand Peruvians. *El lugar de la memoria*, part structure, part infrastructure, digs deeply into its rugged terrain, as if to resist not only the erosion of ground but of memory itself. Carefully inserted into the cliffs and ravines of the arid coastal section of Lima, the architecture becomes one with its terrain, appearing at times as a continuation of the cliffs or as an indispensable retaining embankment. These site strategies integrate the building with its location while camouflaging it along a littoral crowded with housing and commercial enterprises of mixed lineage, all vying for lucrative views of the Pacific Ocean. *El lugar de la memoria* incorporates the sea as an ode to memory and healing, strategically framing the Pacific's majestic blue-gray body as integral to the building's narrative. From the moment visitors enter the four-level structure via a set of interior-exterior ramps and promenades, the sea is experienced in episodic pauses along their itinerary. Sometimes the sea appears to be an immense mirror, sometimes an intimate wedge between the ravine, the building, and the sky. These experiences unfold as visitors descend from, or ascend to, the roof terrace. The terrace is where the sea and sky converge in one prolonged, liberating pause, allowing visitors to ignite a sense of meaning or a spark of hope, as the Pacific Ocean bequeaths its murmuring tranquility.

In 2016 I presided over the jury of the inaugural edition of the Oscar Niemeyer Prize. My colleagues and I unanimously concluded that *El lugar de la memoria* was ideal for the first conferral of this important prize. In addition to the building's architectural merits, it seemed appropriate that an institution dedicated to the preservation of memory should be both a place of reckoning and a solemn warning to prevent the recurrence of such atrocities. In safeguarding and exhibiting the painful memories of Peru's recent past, the place invites reflection on the convulsive history of Latin America. At the time I noted that the building's strength derives from the honesty of its exposed concrete construction. The tough exterior protects the place's internal atmospheric choreography of uplifting spaces, anchored to, yet not weighed down by, their surroundings. El Lugar de la Memoria impresses on first sight as a constructed formation that complements the monolithic materiality of the cliffs. In one sense a raw modern fortification, it also opens to reveal the timeless profile of its shoreline. These experiential contractions and expansions synchronize with specific programmatic intentions. They offer visitors spaces in which to reconcile the brutal and unflinching reality of a wounded past with the possibilities of a more humane future. In the early evening, as the light is extinguished by the deep Peruvian night, the place remains a defiant beacon, where memory refuses to forget.

Early in 2015 I was able to visit El Lugar de la Memoria with my students from Rice University just before the building opened to the public. Because the displays had not yet been installed, the interior volumes possessed the mesmerizing power of emptiness. Combined with the vigilance of the Pacific Ocean, emptiness allowed us to read the structure's spatial organization while sensing the telluric strength of its architecture. One feels that the building belongs to the earth as it springs from the earth. One also feels that the building is nurtured by the earth, an essential element in the alchemy of earth, sea, and sky. These characteristics can be found in other works by Barclay & Crousse: the exquisitely austere Paracas Museum (2008) and the four terraced Vedoble Houses (2011).

These two works are so intertwined with their desert and coastal settings that the effect is startling and reassuring at the same time.

Since completing El Lugar de la Memoria, Barclay & Crousse have continued to explore, assuage, and trace the indomitable topography of their beloved Peru. The formal and material confidence of their works is guided by their mastery of the building section, evident in any of the cross or longitudinal sections cut through the place. A recent academic building for the Universidad de Piura (2016) displays their mastery of section in its compact horizontality. Working in the hot, dry, sun-drenched desert of northern Peru, Barclay & Crousse produced convivial, shaded spaces intent on enriching the collective lives of students. The beauty of this tree-like canopy summons the surrounding forest of carob trees as El lugar de la memoria summons the Pacific Ocean. In 2018 the building in Piura was awarded the Mies Crown Hall Americas Prize. This latest accolade augurs well for Barclay & Crousse as they pursue their daring and admirable course, which mines ancient and contemporary memories of place. It bodes well that they produced a landmark such as El Lugar de la Memoria, which in its sophisticated resolution and materiality embodies a more humane and persuasive modernity.

Carlos Jiménez

General plan

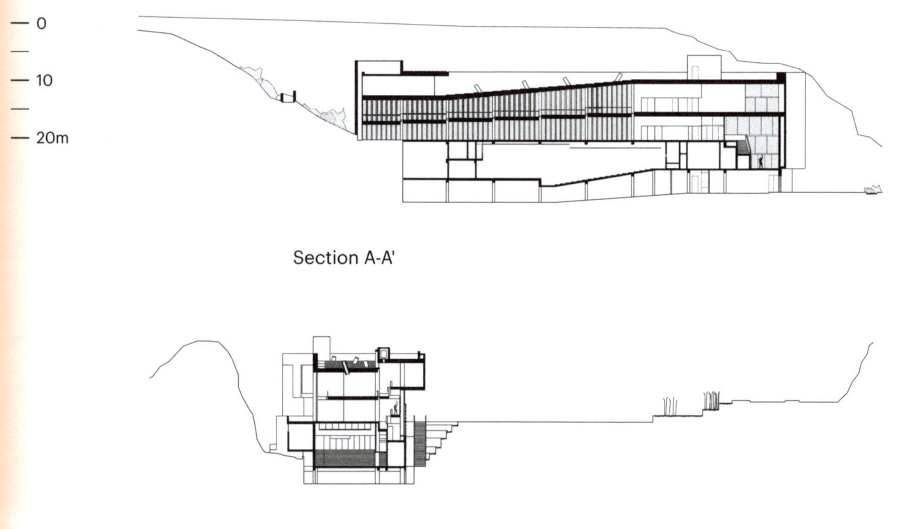

Section A-A'

Section B-B'

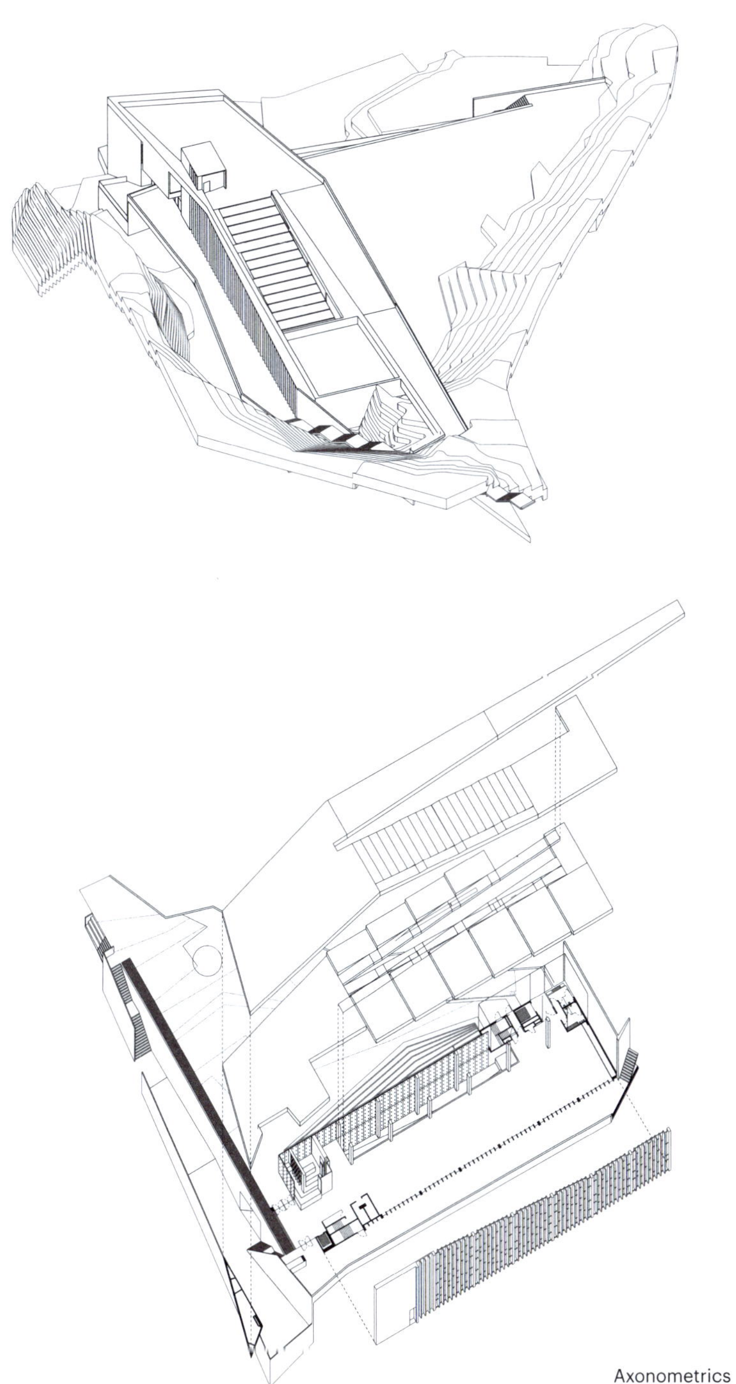

Axonometrics

CURVA
CURVA

CON BALAS

Archivo General del Estado de Oaxaca

Emotion and Restraint

An old professor of mine used to say that it was important to be able to look at the plan of a building for ten minutes or more without the feeling that you were wasting your time.[1] As an architecture student (because that is what I still am), I perform the test with a section, hand-drawn by Ignacio Mendaro Corsini, which passes through the main lobby of the building in which the Archivo General del Estado de Oaxaca are housed. In fact, it is a drawing that contains the section: a fragment of the floor plan and another of the elevation. The section drawn by Mendaro reveals both the shadows and the texture of the materials proposed, but the definition of the pencil strokes blurs toward the center of the drawing. The same occurs with the material of the walls and the saw-tooth roof. Mendaro seems to suggest the rest, without fully drawing it in, as if that were not necessary. And in fact, we can fill it out in our heads. Something similar occurs with his architecture.

That feeling of wasting time mentioned by Professor Helio Piñón not only does *not* arise with Mendaro's section; we feel certain of

1 See Helio Piñón, "Ejercicio 6," in *Curso básico de proyectos* (Barcelona: Edicions Universitat Politècnica de Catalunya, 1998), p. 137.

gaining time, inasmuch as we perceive its presence in the drawing. If we were to attribute one quality to the saw-tooth roof, it would be that of time, because its outline is made perceptible by the changing light of the sun. Gaining time, acquiring it, making it one's own, and putting its cycles to use have always been qualities of the finest architecture. That is what Mendaro is referring to, in part, when he speaks about emotion.

I am looking now at the fragment of the elevation of the threshold into the lobby: two leaves of a steel pivot door, extending horizontally and seemingly impenetrable, beneath heavy concrete cladding. In spite of the singularity of the door, what both body and mind seek out when one visits the building is the changing penumbra of the lobby behind these great doors, which recall a bank vault: the sensation of safekeeping is absolute. In this sense Mendaro seems to be quoting Arne Jacobsen and his National Bank in Denmark, where the heavy opaque door leads into a lobby with the aura of a cathedral, owing to the crosswise filtering of sunlight from above. The comparison is not so far-fetched, if we understand that the two buildings are closed to the exterior and that both safeguard valuables, however different in nature. Mendaro's building is consistent with the appearance it projects from the outside: the massiveness of the concrete walls convey the idea of protecting something valuable, and the architecture is meant to express that. To be and to seem to be.

In contrast to Jacobsen's bank in Copenhagen, where a modern grammar called for symmetry and modular repetition, Mendaro has chosen here a formal diversity nearer to that of a medieval fortress. Something similar can be observed in certain drawings and designs by Julio Cano Lasso, with whom Mendaro collaborated for almost ten years, and from whom he may have acquired a taste for buildings characterized by their solidity and volumetric heterogeneity. One has only to look at the Satellite Communications Center in Buitrago de Lozoya (1966-1967) or the drawings of the three proposals for the main offices of Telefónica on Calle Fuentelarreina (1968, 1973, and 1976), in which Cano Lasso recreates structures whose geometrical richness mirrors that of the surrounding landscape, recalling drawings from his travel notebooks of Spanish towns with deep historical roots.

In the case of Oaxaca, while the building shows the formal diversity to which I have alluded, it is the materials that lend cohesion and harmony to the whole. Its architectural grammar is based on the repetition of certain elements: saw-tooth roofing with different orientations, long stretches of façade with latticework, or solid vertical wall faces that close out a volume. The diversity is not simply an interplay of pleasing shapes: this landscape of volumes is a reflection of the spatial richness of the interior program. An examination of the general plan of the building attests to this abundance, which inevitably recalls the fragmented character of an old town. This aspect of the building, along with the fact that it can be traversed freely, as any visitor will quickly realize, and its function as a piece of pluvial infrastructure, owing to its connection with the quarries and aquatic landscape of the Ciudad de las Canteras, confirm how closely it belongs its particular location.

Like his drawings, which suggest but do not entirely define, Mendaro's architecture calls to mind the atmosphere of the colonial convents and monastic houses in the state of Oaxaca, without falling into the trap of formal literalness. Paradoxically, Mendaro evokes the aura of these spaces through the use of an almost industrial contemporary language. To provoke emotion with good manners requires a certain degree of restraint.

Alejandro Guerrero G.

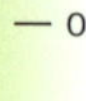

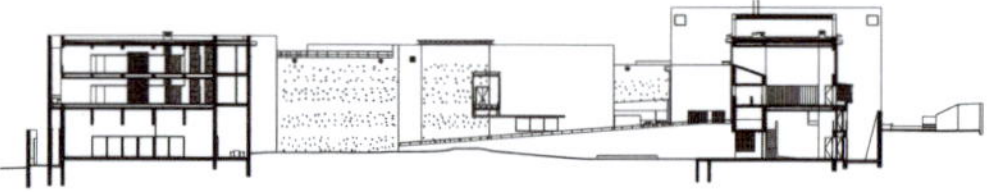

Section A-A'

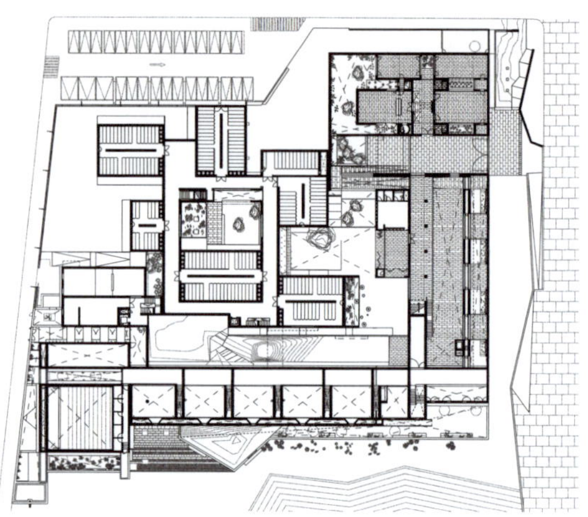

Level 1

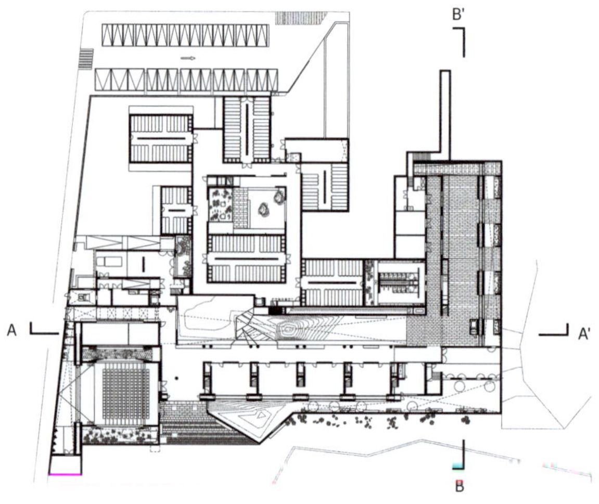

Ground floor plan

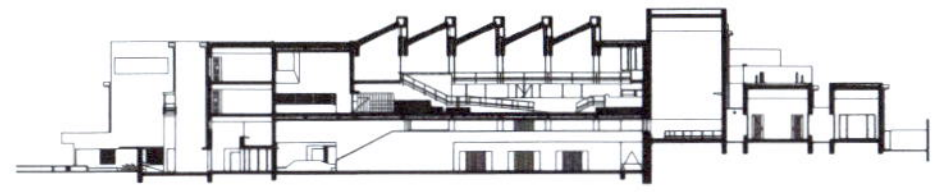

Section B-B'

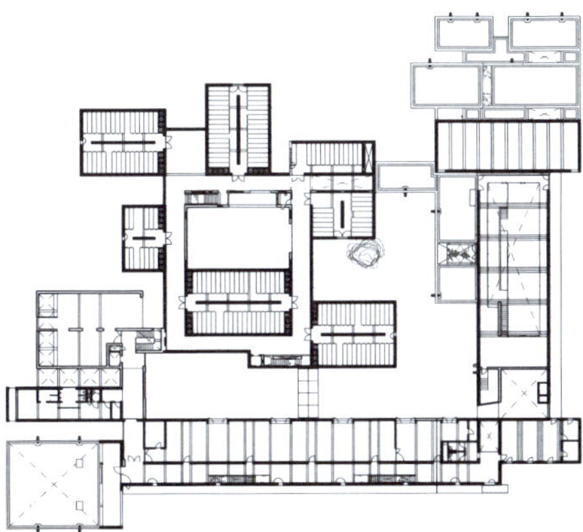

Level 3

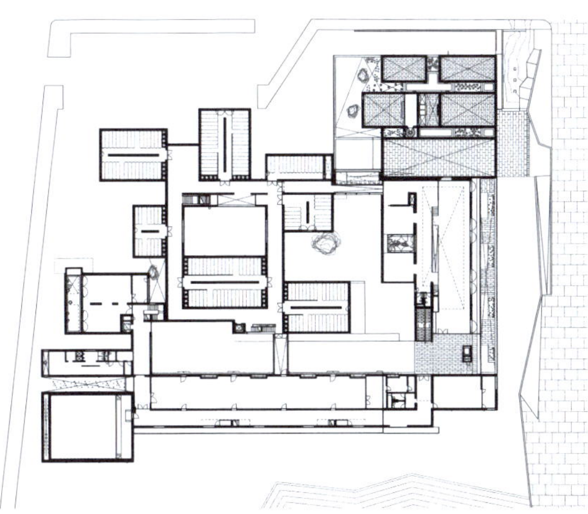

Level 2

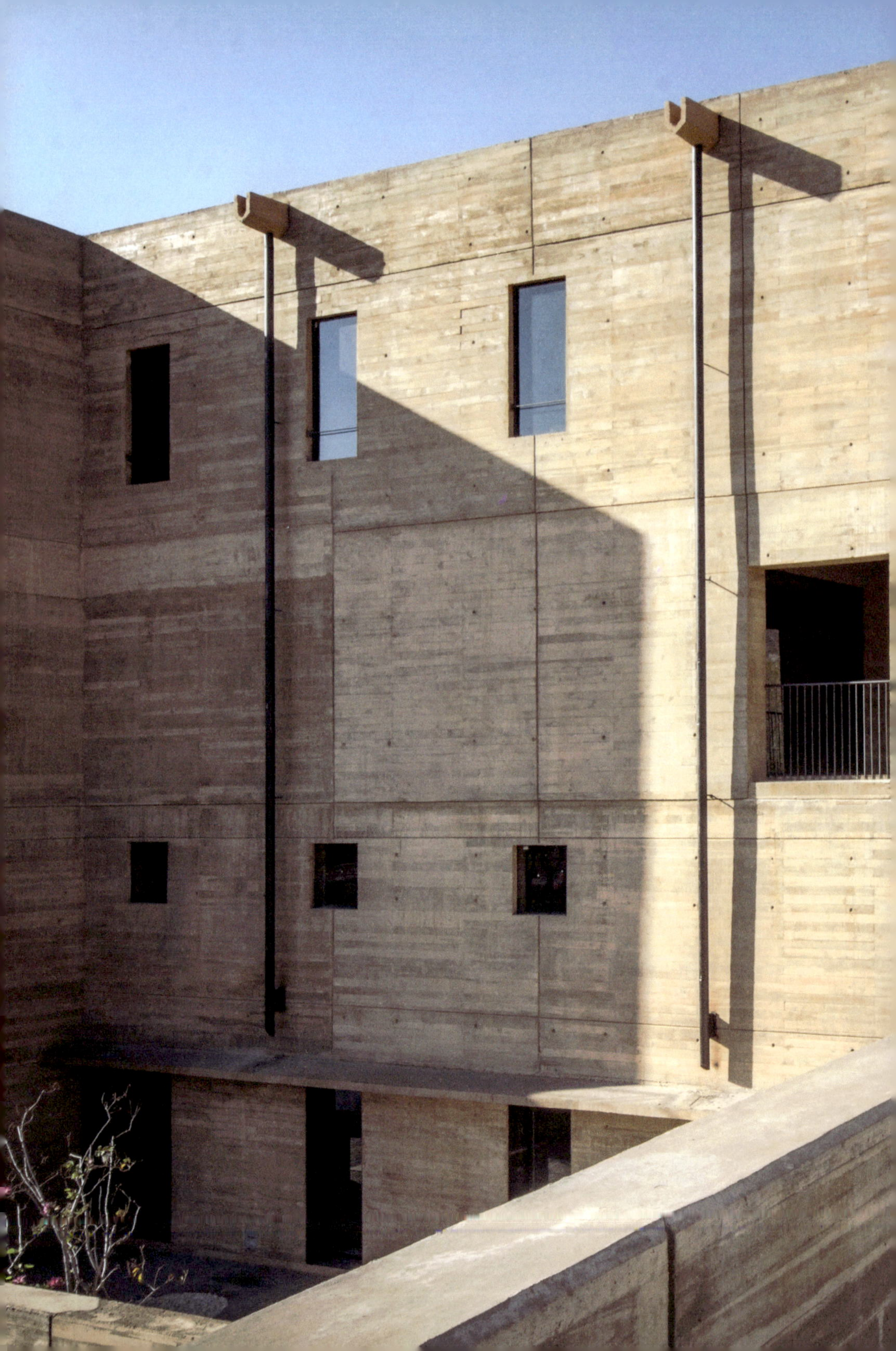

SESC 24 de Maio

In a theoretical design of 2000, Paulo Mendes da Rocha drew the section of a public swimming pool to be built along Praça da República in São Paulo. The pool, supported by two poster-pillars and a group of concrete beams, was to be a container of activities in the center of the largest city in South America. His utopian proposal for an enormous elevated urban beach was the sign of an idea: the collective swimming pool of the Serviço Social do Comércio (SESC) 24 de Maio. On a sunny day, with people swimming or sunbathing amidst the rooftops of the Centro Novo of São Paulo, the realization of this emblematic sketch can be appreciated not simply as a transposition in scale, but as a civic proposal.

The design of the SESC 24 de Maio project is contemporary with the sketch of the pool on Praça da República, but it was not finally constructed until 2017. Mendes da Rocha executed the work in collaboration with MMBB, the firm of Marta Moreira and Milton Braga. The architectural parti always involved the use of the existing building. From the very first sketches, the swimming pool was to crown the building, while an ample program would be distributed vertically, establishing a conscious connection with the urban context.[1]

1 Marta Moreira has recounted that the proposal to create a swimming pool on the roof of the building —in reference to the sketch of the Piscina da República and the design for SESC Tatuapé (1996, but never constructed), both by Mendes

Paulo Mendes da Rocha + MMBB Arquitetos

São Paulo, Brazil, 2017

The SESC is a private institution, affiliated with the Confederação Nacional do Comércio and originally created to serve workers and businesspeople of the goods and services and tourism sectors. The social role of the institution and its centrality in the construction and administration of public equipment outgrew its original purpose and it now attends a wider public, including non-members, through its cultural programs and accessible spaces.

The architectural program of a SESC building is always highly complex and multifunctional. Sporting, recreational, cultural, and health-care activities and services coexist in the same building. The programmatic demands of the institution are clear and are repeated in all of its units, but there is freedom regarding the choice of architectural design and language. From issues of urban scale to details about furnishings, a SESC building embraces all aspects of design and is the closest thing there is to a "total" project in the context of contemporary Brazilian architecture.[2]

da Rocha in collaboration with MMBB— was chosen on the basis of the earliest drawings (Interview with Marta Moreira, May 2021).

2 An exemplary design, on just such a scale and with just such a complex program, is the SESC Pompeia, by Lina Bo Bardi, which began to be constructed in 1997 and was inaugurated in 1986.

The SESC 24 de Maio is part of an important urban fabric, located as it is between Praça da República and the Theatro Municipal de São Paulo. Given the configuration of the city center and its cultural significance, this is crucial to the spatial configuration of the building itself. With the construction of the viaducts along the Vale do Anhangabaú in the late nineteenth and early twentieth centuries, the historic downtown of São Paulo expanded westward to create the Centro Novo. This "new downtown" became a cultural magnet with the creation of the Theatro Municipal and an important commercial district, the setting for a nascent modernity in the city, associated with urban life and consumer society. As large department stores began to occupy corner locations, commercial galleries cut into city blocks and sidewalks were widened for display windows. The Centro Novo exemplified an ideal of urban permeability through architecture, offering an uninterrupted experience from street to interior, with constructions such as the Galeria do Rock, the Copan building, the Itália building, the Galeria Metrópole, and the Galeria das Grandes Galerias, among others.

The main tower of the SESC 24 de Maio has been adapted from a preexisting structure, which housed a now defunct department store in the 1940s.[3] The drastic renovation proposed by Mendes da Rocha was to construct a concrete tower on four pillars over what had been the central void of the former department store. This changed the spatial configuration from that of a building with a perimeter to that of a tower with a free plan. The structural core articulates the principal spaces of the program. On the underground level, without interference from the foundations of the original building, theater audiences occupy the square delimited by the four pillars. The double-height spaces of the entrance lobby

3 The original building, designed by Augusto Rendu, was the regional headquarters of Mesbla. The store occupied the bottom floors and the administrative offices the upper floors. The company ceased operations in 1999.

and the exhibition and sporting areas allow for visual links to be established between floors occupied by the same activities. On top of the building, an elevated volume supports the swimming pool and the changing rooms, creating a gap between the original rooftop and the new structure and making room for a café and garden area, with lateral reflecting pools running alongside.

On his first visit to the site, Mendes da Rocha suggested to the director of the SESC, Danilo Miranda, that he acquire a vacant office tower adjacent to the department store. This could be used to house the services, technical areas, plumbing installations, and machinery, so that the greater part of the main tower could serve functions directly related to the activities of the SESC 24 de Maio. The ramps the connect the floors have been inserted between the two towers. As a continuation of the urban space created by the galleries and sidewalks of the Centro Novo, the ramps allow users to access all of the floors freely, extending the possibility of chance encounters from the street into the interior space. The building also contains open spaces similar to plazas. One is at street level, forming a transition between city and building. The other, called the Garden, is on the former rooftop level, where the café and reflecting pool are located, and offers views of the surrounding buildings of the city center. A third plaza constitutes an informal meeting area: an urban balcony that emerges from the section of the glass façade.

The Garden, or elevated patio, was conceived in relation to the surrounding cityscape. The café is delimited by a reflecting pool which puts some distance between users and the outer limits of the building. The reflecting pool has become an extension of the leisure activities offered by the swimming pool above it, with both children and adults using it to wade in. In a lecture for the Architectural League, architect Marta Moreira explained how this use of the space was not foreseen: it constituted an example of free appropriation by the public for its own enjoyment.[4] In an interview with Giacomo Pirazzoli, Mendes da Rocha described the SESC 24 de Maio project in the following way:

It is an interior and at the same time a machine for discovering the world with one's eyes, creating dialogues with the urban landscape

4 "MMBB Arquitetos and Brasil Arquitetura: Regenerating Downtown São Paulo," The Architectural League (21 May 2021), at https://www.youtube.com/watch?v=-biobgKlrMQE.

near and/or far away. Moreover, the horizontality of the compacted space of the Garden patio is a device that induces people to look outwards, toward the city. This building was designed from the inside out. That is different from the authorial practice of some architects, who seek, in a way, for their signatures to be recognizable.[5]

Sol Camacho

5 "Paulo Mendes da Rocha: sobre o edifício SESC 24 de Maio" [interview with Giacomo Pirazzoli], *Vitruvius* 19 (2018), at https://vitruvius.com.br/revistas/read/entrevista/19.075/7107?page=2.

0

10m

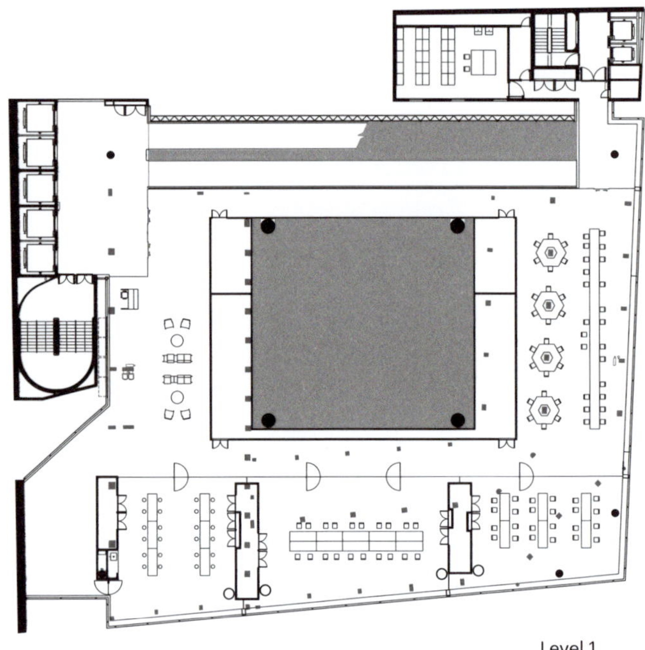

Level 1

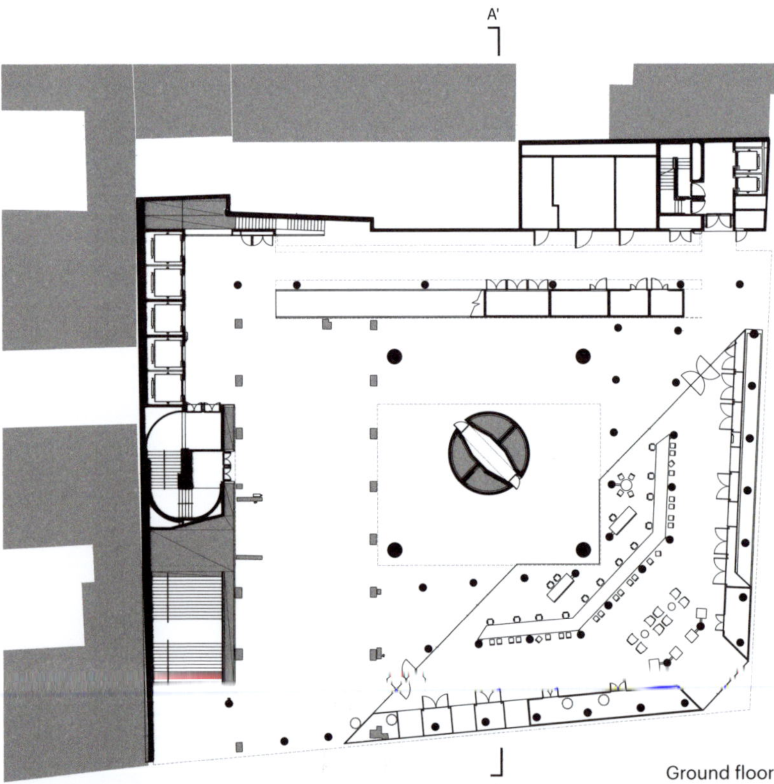

Ground floor plan

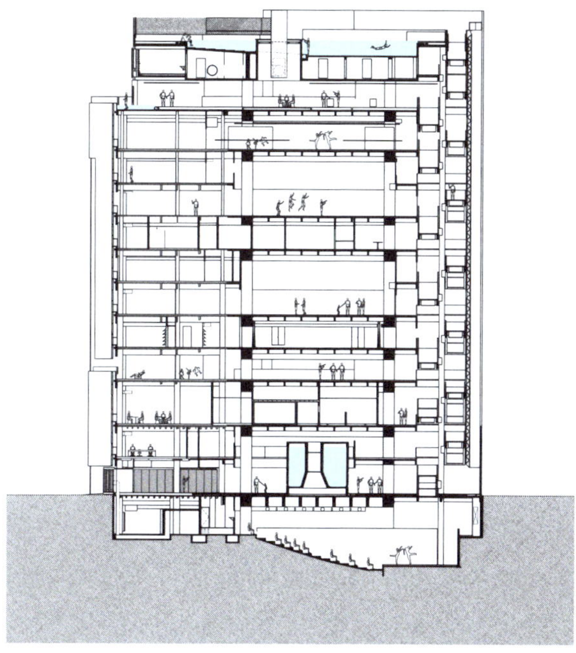

Section A-A'

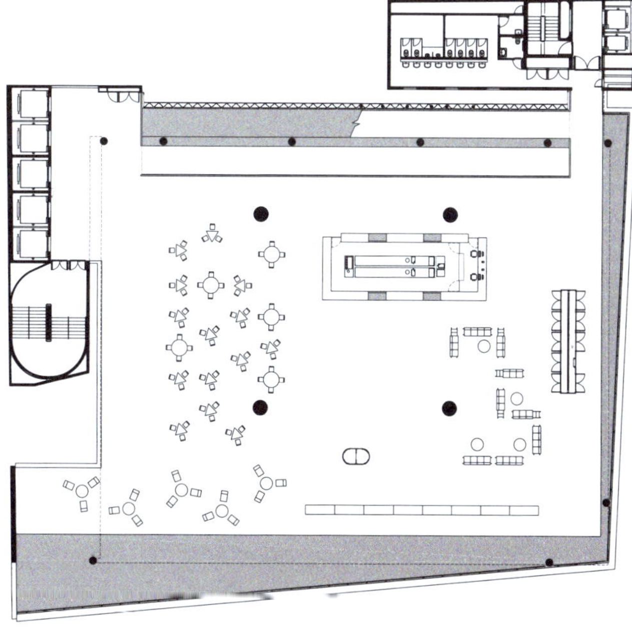

Level 2

Centro Cultural Teopanzolco

Teopanzolco, Beyond the Aerial View

So it is: an inclined volume with a triangular plan looks directly across at an ancient pyramid. Seen from the air, or in the limpid abstraction of a drawing, the design of the Centro Cultural Teopanzolco may be perceived simply as a demonstration of the architects' strict approach. So schematic as almost to be obvious. All this is a confession of my own prejudices, rather than an introduction. We all know the excesses to which architecture is prone, as it simplifies images and diagrams in an attempt to convince.

For a new building even to approach the vestiges of anything we consider a heritage site is always a delicate operation. The taboo of the untouchable is also the context for projects such as the one we are dealing with here. Approaching pre-Hispanic ruins is an feat of audacity that a project can rarely get away with, as demonstrated by so many site museums, which would do better in their endeavor to "dialogue" with the past by simply disappearing. This confirms, perhaps, that learning the deepest lessons of these places is an exercise still rarely undertaken. What ancient Mesoamerican cities have left us as lessons for Mexican architecture, both modern and contemporary, has more to do with the construction of a territory than with a collection of geometrical resources. Xochicalco,

Isaac Broid + PRODUCTORA
Cuernavaca, Mexico, 2017

Cantona, Monte Albán, La Quemada (the list is long) have all bequeathed us something: the lesson that the first step in inhabiting a territory is to mold it. The first stratum that is designed is the empty space on which the architecture is placed.

Since excavating was out of the question, the lot of the Centro Cultural has been gently raised to the highest point permitted, namely, the level of the main temples dedicated to Tláloc and Huitzilopochtli on the base of the archeological site. In accordance with the best pre-Columbian teachings, at this level the visitor gains a perspective on the valley that renders it a connection with the wider place, and not just the immediate surroundings. The landscape can be scanned at many pre-Columbian sites, as it can also be at Teopanzolco, although now it is often the electrical infrastructure, the parking areas, the makeshift urban surroundings —which also constitute an environment— that are the first things one sees. Another confession is in order: it still makes me anxious to see how the two great triangular planes touch in the plaza. In the experience of walking, there is an uncomfortable moment in which someone in the plaza must, literally, *jump the line*.

This topographical transformation, this reinvention of the terrain, succeeds in producing at the same time interior space and a generous amount of fresh stony comfort. If one only looks at images, it is easy to object to the harsh sunlight on the yellowish plaza. But this objection is met by visiting the site after sunset or by occupying the lobby area. Thanks to the diagonals produced by the triangular geometry, the exterior light, always intense in the city of Cuernavaca, filters in through excavated interiors. Within the earthy-colored concrete, the softer tones of wood predominate. In the absence of glass, the site and its air —redolent of springtime— crisscross the project, accentuating its subterranean nature. The sequence ends in the main portico, framing the main temples and, to the north, in a more intimate plaza, a small pelota court, with a pair of preexisting trees, like most of those inserted in this new topography. The main auditorium, which appears closed, is in fact surrounded by open forums.

We must not forget that the Centro Cultural Teopanzolco is a public work. In the Mexican context, this means an arduous defense of the arguments of the original design in the face of shortened calendars and reduced budgets. With the right allies, like the very federal authorities responsible for the heritage sites, for example, this tension can be fortunately resolved, though it may entail a certain rawness in the finishes, which also make a public building both feasible and lasting under our conditions. In addition to the technical challenges of a project with so complex an architectural program, there is also the correct acoustical behavior of the main hall, the impossibility of laying deep foundations, owing to the restrictions on excavating, and the preexistence of a much more precarious auditorium at the outset: its own "former temple," buried in the foundations of the building, waiting perhaps to be unearthed by some future archeologists.

In the face of the strong image projected by this design of Isaac Broid and PRODUCTORA, it may seem out of place to recall the brilliant essay by Ignasi de Solà-Morales on weak architecture, which does not display itself as aggressive or domineering. Nevertheless, the reflections of the Catalan master on the idea of archeology —understood through literature and philosophic thought— allow us to observe Teopanzolco more clearly:

Because, in effect, the experience of certain recent architectures is the experience of superposition. Meaning is not constructed through order, but rather through pieces that possibly end up touching each other; that sometimes approach, without touching; that are close together without ever meeting; that are superposed; or that are displayed in a discontinuity in time which, read as juxtaposition, is the best approximation we can possibly be given in reality.[1]

It is impossible for the pieces to touch. Let us hope that the railing that separates the two structures, the ocher concrete and the ancient stone, will soon disappear, so that their paradoxical proximity may be all the more emphasized.
The importance of this project resides in the opportunity it offers to connect with our built heritage and its teachings in intelligent, attentive, and assertive ways. The collaboration between PRODUCTORA and Isaac Broid has produced something noteworthy: a negotiation with a series of complex tensions and variables —contextual, economic, technical, even political— that have been harmonized in an elegant and sufficient equation. In the economy of lines, the strong gestures, there is still room for certain finesses and for a lively articulation of the settled memories of our historical monuments and the unstable fluidity of our contemporary cities.

Víctor Alcérreca

1 Ignasi de Solà-Morales, *Diferencias. Topografía de la arquitectura contemporánea*, (Barcelona: Editorial GG, 1998), p. 75.

General plan

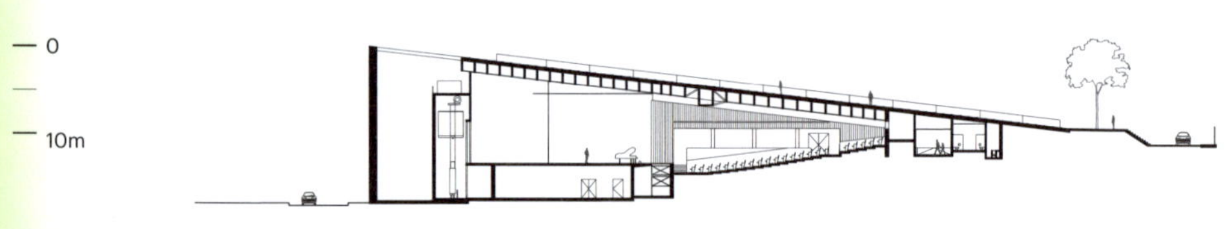

Section A-A'

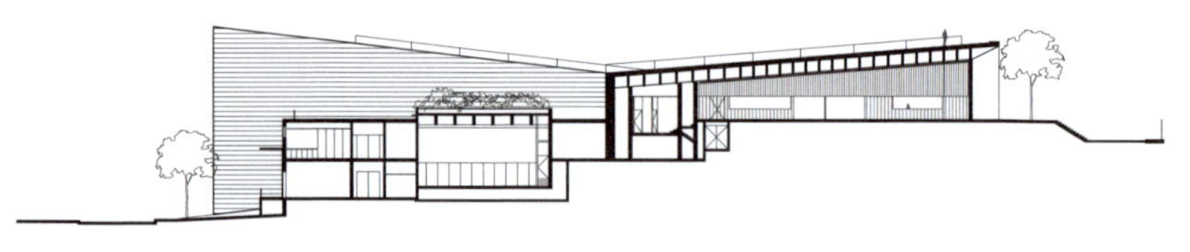

Section B-B'

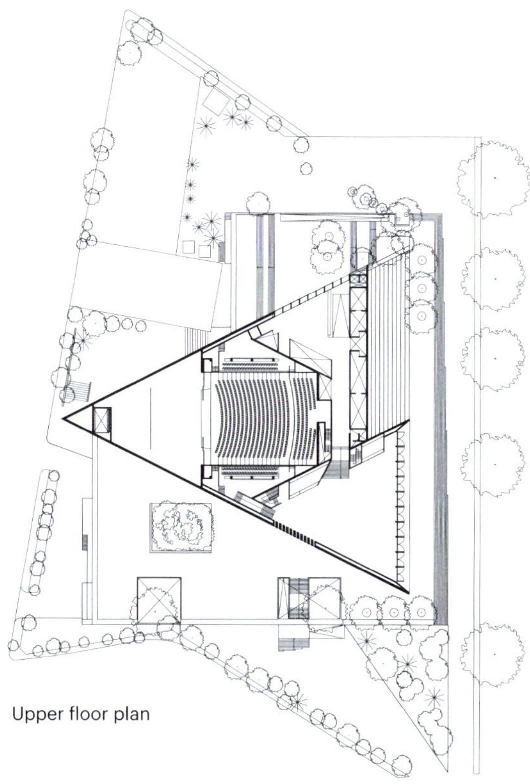

Upper floor plan

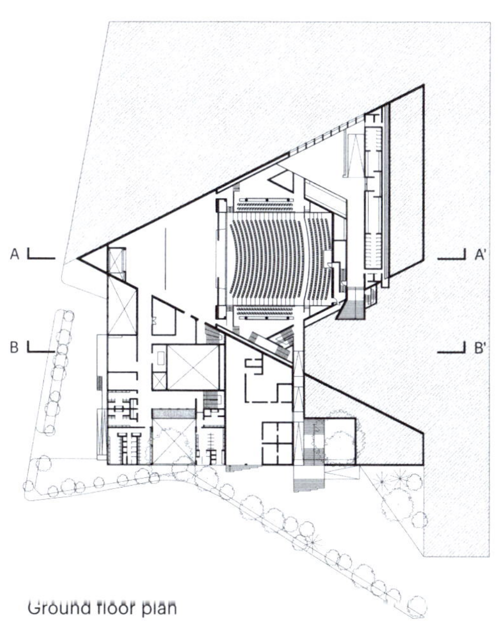

Ground floor plan

Teatro Regional del Biobío

A few months ago, on the occasion of the Trienal Sur del Mundo, in Concepción, Chile, I had the opportunity to visit the Teatro Regional del Biobío. I was just in Concepción for the day, with my afternoon free. I took advantage of being there to ask the organizers of the event if they could arrange for me to visit the theater, which I had found very appealing in photographs I had seen.

The first thing that struck me was the scale of the work. In spite of the immense emptiness of the surroundings, the theater is able to project itself as a structure of large dimensions, with a strong presence, without conveying a sense of monumentality. The second thing that impressed me was its spatial relationship to the 27F Memorial. Together they create a space that functions naturally as an atrium for the theater. Finally, the volumetric layout and the texture of the building's skin, resting on countless slanted, triangulated columns, reminded me of the subtle blends of Kazuyo Sejima's architecture and the structural explorations of Christian Kerez.

Upon entering, the sense is one of surprise, on discovering that the orthogonal structural grid is endlessly repeated. The experience is like walking within an artificial mathematical organism. It is a sort of game that keeps adapting itself to the programmatic and spatial requirements. Since the building's transparency, and therefore its relation to the exterior, is strictly defined, walking through it is like being inside a body, without perimeter walls. The opaque bodies are toward the center: rooms and support services covered by large mantles. The interior of the rooms is another surprise. After passing through the rather dense structural forest, one enters these immense empty black spaces, very abstract, neutral, and lacking in visual information.

On the plane back to Santiago, we passed just four hundred meters above the theater. It was getting dark and I saw that, in effect, the building functions as a sort of lamp for the city of Concepción. The series of encounters with the work, in the course of just one afternoon, from different points of view, moved me deeply as an architect. It occurred to me that it might be one of those buildings to be visited by anyone interested in exploring the nature and power of architecture.

In the following days, I remembered a design by Smiljan Radic, dating from around 1986, which won the CAP competition for architecture students, in an edition presided by Horacio Borgheresi. It was a gymnasium with a metallic structure, highly Cartesian, the volume of the building rotated a few degrees with respect to the structure itself. I also recalled something of the inflatable structure with which he took part in the celebration of the architecture school's 90th anniversary. The notion of a minimal, translucent skin was an almost chance discovery in his second year of university. In the

Teatro Regional de Biobío, the structural exploration and the subtlety of a minimal skin come together, constants that have been of interest to Smiljan Radic from an early age.

Mathias Klotz

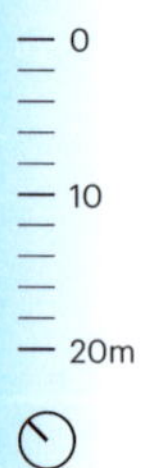

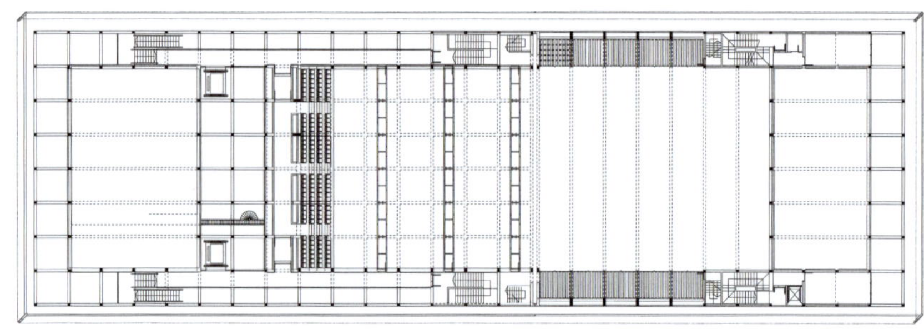

Level 2

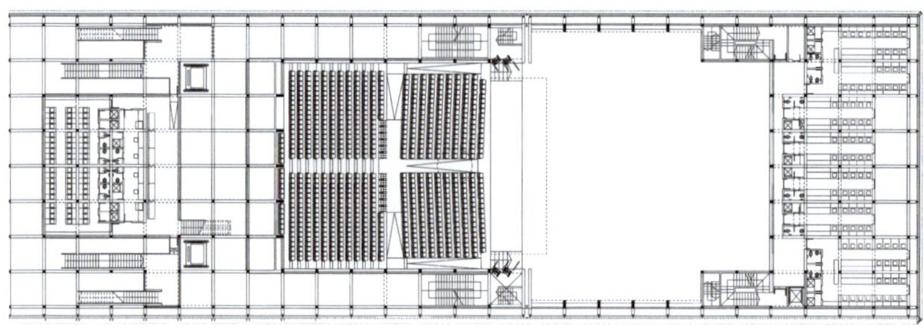

Level 1

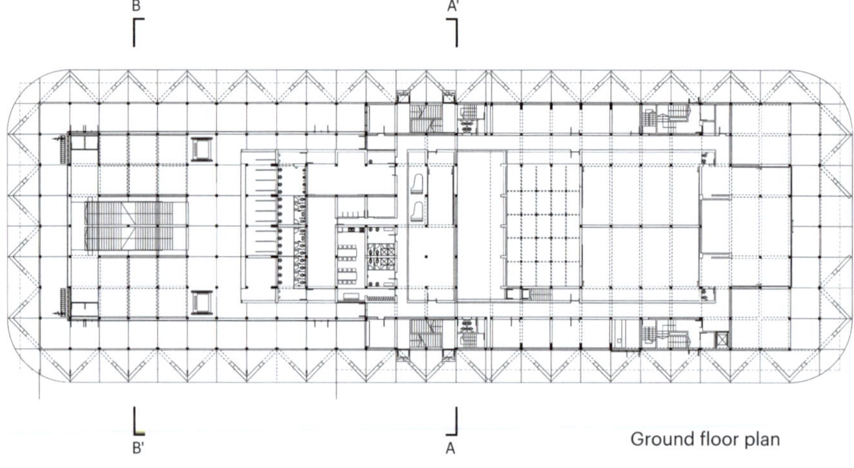

Ground floor plan

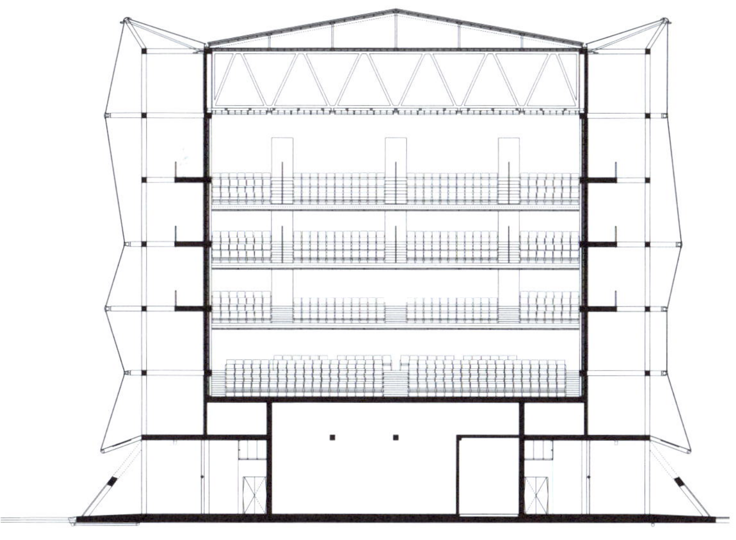

Section A-A'

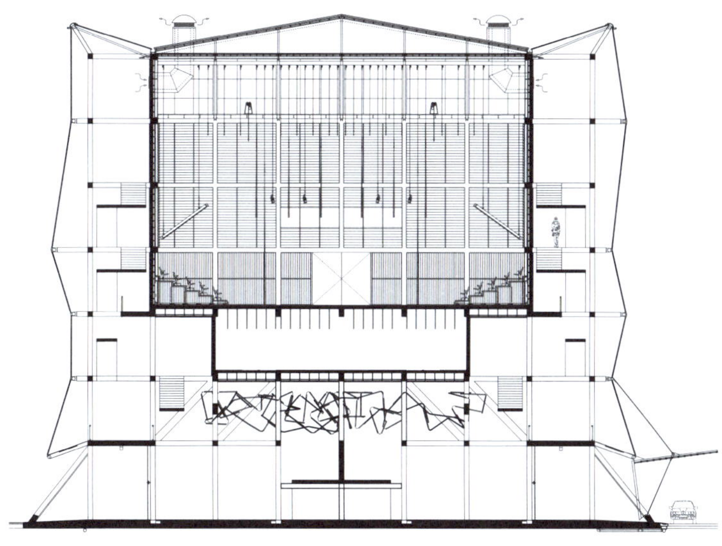

Section B-B'

Palacio Pereira

Strategies of Coexistence

The Palacio Pereira by Cecilia Puga, Paula Velasco, and Alberto Moletto is not a palace in the strict sense. It is neither a residence for royalty nor an opulent mansion for the wealthy and the eminent. Neither is it the family seat of some aristocratic line or a place where monarchs granted public audiences. The Pereira, as the architects call it, is more than a palace: it is many buildings in one. It is difficult to define it or put a label on it within conventional parameters. Above all, it is a sum of real and virtual elements in coexistence, some of them obvious and others concealed from the eyes of users. The fact that it continues to be called a "palace" suggests the participation of different ages —what it is and what is has been— and is an explicit declaration of an alliance between conservation and renovation.

The Pereira is a complex building, of a kind not common in Chile, in which different layers, compromises, interests, programs, and authors have accumulated and are displayed. It is definitely a work that restores to the building its fundamental role in the discipline, as well as making it a topic of discussion outside of the realm of architecture per se, of relevance to issues related to the city, to public and social life, and above all to politics.

Cecilia Puga + Paula Velasco + Alberto Moletto
Santiago, Chile, 2019

In the Pereira different agents and wills coexist, and that is one of its virtues. After actually being a palace, through the nineteenth and early twentieth centuries it changed ownership several times, was abandoned, was turned into a school, and later even housed artists' studios and was a venue for underground cultural events. It then fell into neglect again, suffering continued deterioration until it was almost a ruin. There were development projects, of no value at all, that proposed reducing it to just a façade, with a tower behind it. In 2011 the Chilean government became involved, purchasing the building with the idea of transforming it into the premises of the federal department responsible for libraries, archives, and museums, and of the Council of National Monuments, which is in charge of safeguarding Chile's built cultural heritage. A single limited program, however, was insufficient and unfeasible from a sociopolitical point of view. It was necessary to expand it and combine it with other public programs, which would open up the building to a wider public. Reading and exhibition rooms were added to the project, along with a café, an auditorium, and a public lobby, created in the transept, which had been perhaps the most iconic space of the former palace. The renovation utterly transformed the usual way of understanding an institutional building.

Chile tends to be a country of short-term initiatives, limited by the duration of presidential administrations. The case of the Pereira is an exception to this, as it has consolidated the political will necessary to the time frame of a building, a public project, or even a country. The competition was organized and the project developed under a center-right government. Construction began during a center-left administration and ended during another center-right one. In short, the building can be understood as public policy.

The team that won the competition —Puga, Velasco, and Moletto— is a partnership of two generations: one which, since the 1990s, has been transforming architectural discourses and the approach to the discipline in Chile, and a second generation largely mentored by the first, albeit with new and updated interests and challenges. This project has had important consequences for its architects. Puga and Velasco have consolidated one of the most outstanding professional and academic partnerships of the last decade in Chile. It is worth mentioning that they went on to win another public competition for the design of the Valparaíso Regional Archives, bringing the ruins of yet another palace —the Subercaseaux this time— back to life again in 2022. Moletto's firm, on the other hand, has solidified a practice that combines private projects and public competitions. The three architects were joined by Alan Chandler and Fernando Pérez, responsible for heritage issues, and a long list of other professionals, which demonstrates that the coexistence of disciplines is not just a slogan, but a fundamental aspect of being able to undertake complex time-consuming commissions.

When the documentation had been analyzed and the site visited, it became evident that this would not be a unitary project. It combined preexisting elements and new proposals, strategies for conservation as well as for renovation. The project would involve spaces with differing degrees of intervention and a variety of solutions, as if there were to be as many architects as buildings, with a range of superposed projects: façade, transept gallery, café and reading room, documentation center, interior exhibition rooms, rooms on the urban front, patio, auditorium, and office block.

This is evident in the materials, in the combination of masonry walls which have lost all their ornamentation and those spaces in which it has been maintained, with both damage and repairs still visible. Some elements have been restored with the highest conservation standards. New materials, such as exposed reinforced concrete, reflective metals, and large panes of glass, have been combined with the original ones.

Structural and constructive systems also coexist in the building. The wall structure that has survived occupies just a part of a larger site, completed by means of a new structure of pillars, jousts, beams, and reinforced concrete slabs, erected around a patio: perhaps the most emblematic gesture of the intervention.

Processes and strategies in architecture often tend to be linear and monothematic, while arguments are artificially coherent. The architects of the Palacio Pereira saw an opportunity to develop and transform the building in a different way: by strategies of coexistence. A building can give new life to a setting or a milieu that is stagnating in its own certitudes.

Guillermo Hevia García

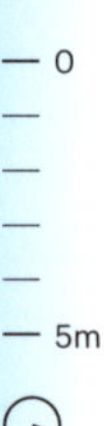

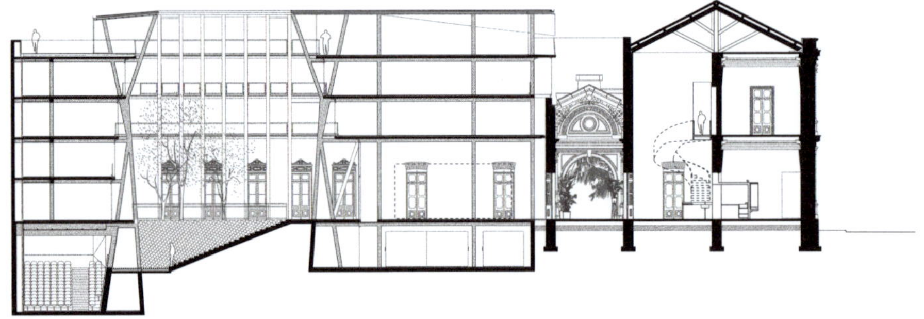

Section A-A'

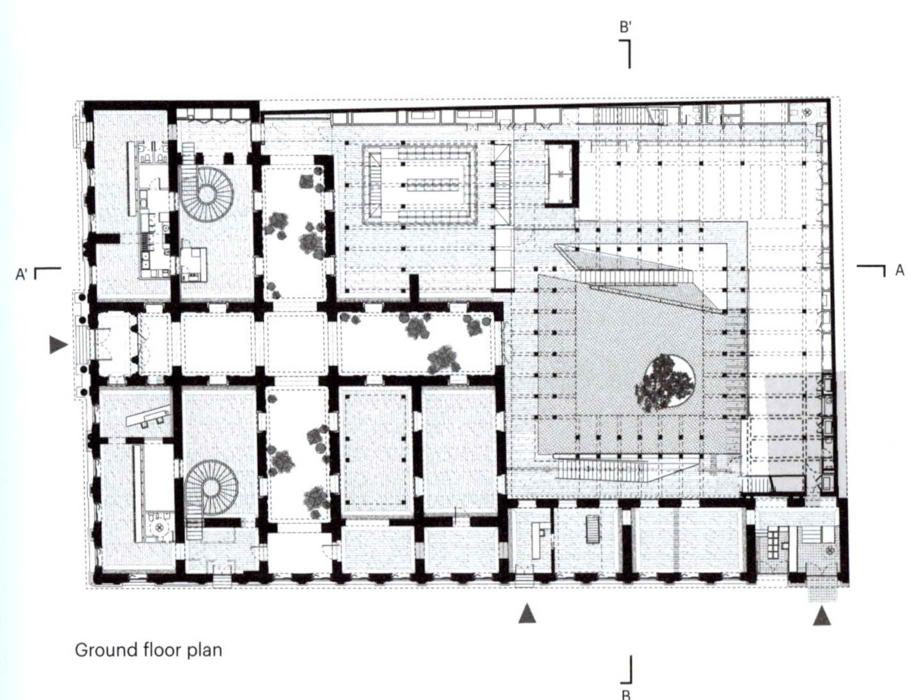

Ground floor plan

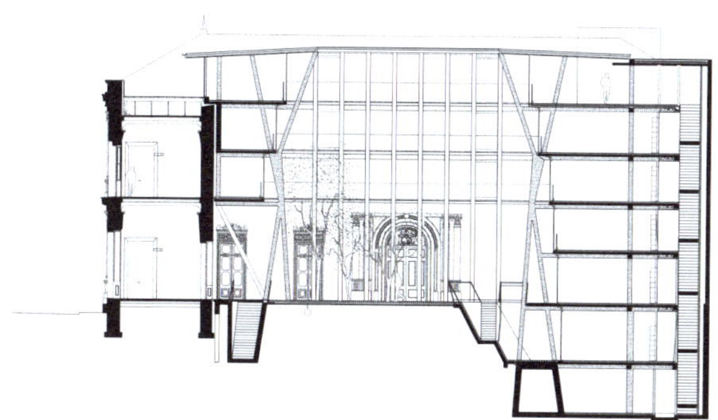

Section B-B'

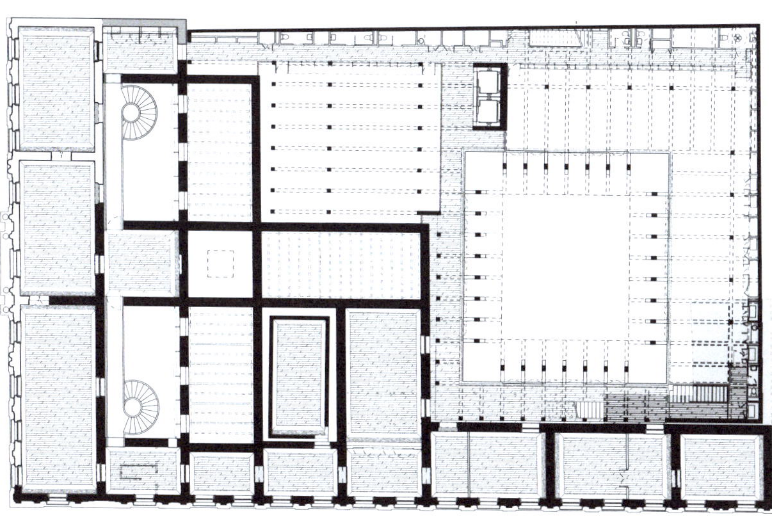

Level 1

About the authors

Al Borde is an Ecuadorian architecture firm founded in 2007 by Pascual Gangotena, David Barragán, Marialuisa Borja, and Esteban Benavides. It has participated in emblematic exhibitions such as *Think Global, Build Social! Architectures for a Better World* (Vienna, 2014) and *Reporting from the Front* at the Venice Architecture Biennial in 2016. The firm is recognized for its ability to offer a response of esthetic and social empowerment in a context of scarcity.

Alberto Moletto is an architect graduated from the Universidad Finis Terrae (Santiago de Chile) in 2000, with an MSc in sustainable environmental design from the Architectural Association School of Architecture (London) in 2009. In England he worked at the firm of Zaha Hadid Architects and was a professor at both the Architectural Association and the University of East London. In 2012 he returned to Chile and established his own firm, focusing on public works and educational projects. He has been invited to present his work at the Escola da Cidade in São Paulo, the Illinois Institute of Technology in Chicago, the University of East London and the Architectural Association, the Tokyo University of Science, the Istituto Universitario di Architettura di Venezia, the Shenzhen Architecture Biennial in China, and Tilburg University in Holland. He currently teaches at the Pontificia Universidad Católica de Chile and the Universidad Finis Terrae.

Alejandro Echeverri is a Colombian architect, the cofounder and director of the Centro de Estudios Urbanos y Ambientales Urbam at the Universidad EAFIT in Medellín. He is also a professor at the school of architecture, art, and design of the Instituto Tecnológico y de Estudios Superiores de Monterrey in Mexico. His professional experience embraces architecture, urbanism, environmental and social projects and processes, and territorial planning. He was worked in these fields privately, as an academic, and through government. Echeverri is a Loeb Fellow at the Harvard Graduate School of Design and was awarded the Obayashi Prize in Japan in 2016 for his work in innovating and revitalizing Medellín and other cities in precarious circumstances around the world.

Alejandro Guerrero G. graduated as an architect from the Instituto Tecnológico y de Estudios Superiores de Occidente and earned a master's degree at the Universitat Politècnica de Catalunya in 2006. He has partnered professionally with Andrea Soto since 2011. He has received the Emerging Voices award of The Architectural League of New York and the Design Vanguard award of *Architectural Record*, as well as a nomination for the Mies Crown Hall Americas Prize. He has lectured at Mantov-Architettura and at the Harvard Graduate School of Design, as part of the Latin GSD lecture series. His two-volume *Arquitecturas del fuego* [Architectures of Fire] was published in 2020.

Alejandro Hernández Gálvez studied architecture. He has participated in the "Mexico City Dialogues" in New York City and in the Rotterdam, São Paulo, Canary Islands, and Venice architecture biennials. He has curated numerous exhibitions and contributed to a wide range of media outlets. He is the co-author of *de 100x100, arquitectos del siglo XX en México* [100x100: Twentieth-Century Architects in Mexico] and the author of *Sombras, sombreros y sombrillas: algunos principios de la arquitectura* [Shadows, Hats, and Umbrellas: Some Architectural Principles]. He has taught at the architecture schools of the Universidad Iberoamericana, CENTRO, and the Instituto Superior de Arquitectura y Diseño, and was visiting professor at the Southern California Institute of Architecture in Los Angeles. He was a member of the Sistema Nacional de Creadores in Mexico for two periods (2007-2010 and 2016-2019). He is the editorial director of Arquine.

Álvaro Siza studied architecture at the Escola Superior de Belas-Artes do Porto in Portugal. He graduated in 1966 and began to work as a professor. He has been visiting professor at Harvard and at universities in Lausanne, Philadelphia, and Bogotá. In 1988 he received the Mies van der Rohe Award (the European Union Prize for Contemporary Architecture), the Medalla de Oro de la Arquitectura (awarded by the Consejo Superior de los Colegios de Arquitectos de España), and the Gold Medal of the Alvar Aalto Foundation. In 1992 he was awarded the Pritzker Prize and in 1998 the Praemium Imperiale of the Japan Art Association.

Andrea Griborio is an architect with two master's degrees —one in criticism and design and the other in the theory and practice of architectural design— from the Escola Tècnica Superior d'Arquitectura de Barcelona (Universitat Politècnica de Catalunya). She has worked with Arquine since 2010, editing several architecture books and coordinating projects such as the Arquine Congress, the magazine's international architecture competition, the Arquine Jams, and the audiovisual interview program *La hora Arquine*. Since 2014 she has been the director of MEXTRÓPOLI | Festival de Arquitectura y Ciudad, which involves more than 50,000 people a year in activities connected with the construction of culture through architecture.

Andrea Soto Morfín is an architect graduated from the Instituto Tecnológico y de Estudios Superiores de Occidente. She has partnered professionally with Alejandro Guerrero since 2011. She was awarded the Marcelo Zambrano architecture scholarship by CEMEX in 2015 to study at the Harvard Graduate School of Design (GSD), from which she graduated with honors and a citation from the American Society of Landscape Architects. She has received the Emerging Voices award of The Architectural League of New York and was nominated for the Mies Crown Hall Americas Prize. She has lectured in the Latin GSD lecture series, at MantovArchitettura, and at the University of British Columbia, and has served as visiting critic at the GSD and the University of Virginia School of Architecture.

AGENdA agencia de arquitectura is a firm founded by Camilo Restrepo Ochoa and Juliana Gallego Martínez in Medellín in 2010. It received the Premio CEMEX 2021 for the best public work of social value in Mexico for the Church and Sanctuary of Our Lord of Tula (in partnership with Dellekamp Schleich) and second place in the awards of the Fondazione Frate Sole in Italy, for the best church built in the world during the period 2016-2020. In 2020, *Domus* included AGENdA on its list of the "50 Best Architecture Firms," alongside some of the world's most influential and creative studios. AGENdA was nominated for the Mies Crown Hall Americas Prize in 2022.

Camilo Restrepo Ochoa is an architect graduated from the Universidad Pontificia Bolivariana in Medellín in 1997, who went on to earn a master's degree in the Metrópolis program of the Universitat Politècnica de Catalunya and the Centre de Cultura Contemporània de Barcelona in 2004-2005. He has been a critic at the Harvard Graduate School of Design from 2013 to 2016 and from 2020 to the present. He was guest editor of the magazine *a+u* (Japan) for its special issue devoted to Colombia.

Barclay & Crousse was founded by Sandra Barclay and Jean Pierre Crousse in Paris. Since 2006 the firm has been established in Lima, Peru, where it has developed private projects along with several works of a public character, proposing daring ideas that stretch the limits of the architectural program and the context: more than making connections with the landscape, their architecture is landscape in itself. The depth of their façades blurs the limits between interior and exterior, and their works explore the potentials of materials while consecrating certain spaces of encounter, where the extraordinary becomes an everyday phenomenon. In 2018 they were awarded the Mies Crown Hall Americas Prize for the E Building of the Universidad de Piura.

Jean Pierre Crousse is an architect, researcher, and professor, with a master's degree in territory and landscape. He is director of the master's program in architecture and design processes at the Pontificia Universidad Católica del Perú and a professor at Harvard, Yale, the École Nationale Supérieure d'Architecture de Paris-Belleville, and the University of Virginia. He was the curator, along with Sandra Barclay, of the Peruvian pavilion at the 15th International Architecture Exhibition of the Venice Biennale, receiving a special mention from the jury.

Bertolino Barrado Arquitectos is a firm made up of Mónica Bertolino and Carlos Barrado, both architects graduated from the Universidad Nacional de Córdoba in Argentina. They have undertaken architectural, urban, and landscape projects of different scales and focuses since 1981. The firm has received numerous distinctions in both Argentina and internationally, including honorable mention at the Premios Konex 2012, the Panorama de Obras of the 8th Bienal Iberoamericana de Arquitectura y Urbanismo, and honorable mention at the Bienal Panamericana de Quito. Both architects are professors in the undergraduate and post-graduate programs of the Universidad Nacional de Córdoba and the Universidad Nacional del Litoral. They have been invited to numerous universities as guest lecturers, as well as to forums, biennials, and congresses in Argentina, the rest of Latin America, the United States, Europe, and South Africa. They are the cofounders of RedSur, a project created in 2009 in the aim of opening up an academic space in Latin America. Their architectural and theoretical work has appeared in numerous media outlets in Argentina and internationally.

Carlos Jiménez was born in San José, Costa Rica, in 1959 and moved to the United States in 1974. He graduated from the Gerald D. Hines College of Architecture at the University of Houston in 1981 and established Carlos Jiménez Studio in 1983. He has been a tenured Professor at the Rice School of Architecture in Houston since 2000, as well as a visiting professor at the Southern California Institute of Architecture, the University of California at Los Angeles and at Berkeley, the Universidad de Navarra in Pamplona Spain, Tulane University in New Orleans, the Harvard Graduate School of Design, the University of Texas at Arlington and at Austin, the University of Oregon, and Washington University in Saint Louis. Jiménez is a frequent lecturer, critic, and jury member at both national and international architecture events. He served on the jury of the Pritzker Architecture Prize from 2001 to 2011.

Cecilia Puga graduated as an architect from the Pontificia Universidad Católica de Chile in 1990. Her work, which ranges over a variety of scales and programs, has been internationally acclaimed, including family residences such as the one in Bahía Azul (Chile), collective housing, educational and industrial projects, urban design projects, such as the renovation of public spaces in Cerro Toro (Valparaíso), and, most recently, the new premises of the Ministry of Cultures, Arts, and Heritage in Santiago de Chile. She currently teaches at the Pontificia Universidad Católica de Chile and has been a visiting professor at the Department of Architecture at ETH Zürich (2017-2019), the school of architecture of the University of Texas at Austin (2015), and the Harvard School of Design (2009), among other institutions. Since 2020, alongside her professional work, she has been director of the Museo Chileno de Arte Precolombino.

Cristóbal Molina Baeza is coordinator of the architecture section of the Chilean Ministry of Cultures, Arts, and Heritage, responsible for plans, programs, and initiatives to promote architecture as a cultural expression. He is an architect with a master's degree and a doctorate, as well as a promoter and researcher specializing in cultural policy, heritage, and international projects. He teaches at the architecture school of the Pontificia Universidad Católica de Chile. He has written several books and curated numerous exhibitions and pavilions, including the Chilean pavilions at the last five editions of the Venice Biennale.

Daniel Bonilla is an architect graduated from the Universidad de Los Andes in Bogotá, with a master's degree in urban design from Oxford Brookes University (1990). He has also studied at the Technological University Dublin and the Politecnico di Milano in Italy. In 1997, following ample professional experience in Bogotá and London, he established his own firm in partnership with the architect Marcela Albornoz, undertaking some significant urban design, architectural, and industrial projects. In 2010 Bonilla founded tab>| Taller de Arquitectura de Bogotá.

David Chipperfield Architects was founded in London by David Chipperfield in 1985. The firm has offices in London, Berlin, Milan, and Shanghai. The practice has won numerous international competitions and developed over a hundred projects, including cultural, residential, commercial, and educational buildings and spaces for both the private and public sectors, as well as civic projects and urban masterplans. David Chipperfield Architects has won more than one hundred international awards and citations for design excellence, including the Stirling Prize of the Royal Institute of British Architects for the Museum of Modern Literature in Marbach, Germany, in 2007, and both the Mies van der Rohe Award (European Union Prize for Contemporary Architecture) and the Deutscher Architekturpreis for the Neues Museum in Berlin in 2011.

ELEMENTAL is a "Do Tank" made up of Alejandro Aravena, Gonzalo Arteaga, Juan Cerda, Victor Oddó, and Diego Torres. Founded in 2001, it focuses on public-interest and social-impact projects such as housing, public space, infrastructure, and transport. ELEMENTAL has constructed in Chile, the United States, Mexico, China, and Switzerland. Alejandro Aravena is an architect graduated from the Pontificia Universidad Católica de Chile in 1992. From 2000 to 2005 he was a professor at Harvard University, where ELEMENTAL was founded in collaboration with Andrés Iacobelli. From 2009 to 2015 Aravena was a member of the jury of the Pritzker Architecture Prize. He was awarded the prize himself in 2016 and appointed director the same year of the 15th International Architecture Exhibition of the Venice Biennale: *Reporting from the Front*.

Elisa Silva has been the director of Enlace Arquitectura since 2007 and of Enlace Fundación since 2017. She has a master's degree in architecture from the Harvard Graduate School of Design (GSD). Her work has been presented and has won awards at the 7th and 11th editions of the Bienal Iberoamericana de Arquitectura y Urbanismo, the 20th edition of the Bienal de Arquitectura in Chile, the Venice Biennale in 2021, Chicago Architecture Biennial in 2021, and at the arc en rêve centre d'architecture in 2022. Silva won the Rome Prize of the American Academy in Rome in 2005 and the Wheelwright Prize of the GSD in 2011. In 2017 and 2021 she was the recipient of a grant from the Graham Foundation. She is the author of *Puro espacio: transformaciones de espacio público en asentamientos espontáneos de América Latina* [Pure Space: Transformations of Public Space in Spontaneous Settlements in Latin America] (Actar, 2020). She has taught at Princeton, the University of Toronto, the Universidad Simón Bolívar, and the GSD. She currently gives classes at Florida International University.

Ernesto Betancourt is an architect graduated from the Universidad Nacional Autónoma de México (UNAM). He designs and develops architectural and urban projects, with a focus on the salvaging of public spaces. His projects include the music conservatory of the Centro Nacional de las Artes and the premises of the Fondo de Cultura Económica, in collaboration with Teodoro González de León, as well as the Paseo de la Reforma and the Parque Urbano La Mexicana. He is currently director of the firm EbgA, which focuses on architectural projects and urban planning. Betancourt has master's degrees in urban planning from the Universidad Iberoamericana (UIA) and the Universitat Politècnica de Catalunya. He is a founding member of Arquine and serves on its editorial board. He has taught at the UNAM, the UIA, and more recently at CENTRO. He is a lifetime member of the Academia Nacional de Arquitectura.

Francisco Díaz is an architect with a master's degree from the Pontificia Universidad Católica de Chile (UC) and a second master's in critical, curatorial, and conceptual practices in architecture from Columbia University in New York. He has also done post-graduate work at the Politecnico di Torino in Italy. An assistant professor at the architecture school of the UC, he has published and lectured both in Chile and around the world, including Australia, Brazil, Ecuador, Spain, the United States, Italy, Macedonia, Peru, and Uruguay. He was the editor-in-chief of Ediciones ARQ and the magazine *ARQ* from 2014 to 2022, responsible for more than one hundred books published and 22 issues of the magazine. His most recent book *Patologías contemporáneas: ensayos de arquitectura tras la crisis* [Contemporary Pathologies: Architecture Essays after the Crisis] (2008) was awarded the prize of the Bienal Española de Arquitectura y Urbanismo in 2021.

Francisco Pardo is an architect with a master's degree in architecture from Columbia University in New York. In Mexico he was a recipient of the "Young Creators" grant of the Fondo Nacional para la Cultura y las Artes in 2001 and has been a member of the Sistema Nacional de Creadores since 2010. In the year 2000 he founded AT103 and in 2016 the firm of Francisco Pardo Arquitecto in Mexico City. In 2009 he received the Emerging Voices award of The Architectural League of New York. His work has been widely published and exhibited in Mexico and abroad and he has been a visiting professor at various international institutions. He is currently a professor at the Southern California Institute of Architecture in Los Angeles, where he coordinates the SCI-Arc Mexico City program.

Frida Escobedo established her architecture and design studio in 2006 in Mexico City. Her work embraces a variety of subjects, from art installation to furniture design, in addition to residences and public buildings. She has received numerous distinctions, including the Architectural League Prize (formerly known as the Young Architect's Forum) in 2009, the award of the Bienal Iberoamericana de Arquitectura y Urbanismo in 2014, the Emerging Architecture Award of *The Architectural Review* in 2016, and the Emerging Voices award of The Architectural League of New York in 2017. She has been a visiting professor at the Columbia University Graduate School of Architecture, Planning and Preservation, the Harvard Graduate School of Design (GSD), and the Architectural Association in London. In the fall of 2017 she was appointed Howard A. Friedman Professor at the University of California at Berkeley and in the spring of 2019 she taught at Rice University in Houston. She currently gives classes at the GSD.

Germán del Sol graduated as an architect from the Pontificia Universidad Católica de Chile and the Escola Tècnica Superior d'Arquitectura de Barcelona. In 1973 he founded his firm in Barcelona and in 1980 moved it to Santiago de Chile. His principal works include the Chilean pavilion at Seville Expo '92 in Spain; the Hotel Explora and bathhouse in Patagonia (in collaboration with José Cruz); the Hotel Explora Atacama at the Puritama hot springs; the stables and the saunas and pools in Atacama; the Viña Gracia de Chile wine storerooms in Totihue; the geometric hot springs near Coñaripe; the Hotel Remota in Patagonia; and the Spa Remota in Puerto Natales, all in Chile.

Giancarlo Mazzanti is an architect and the founder of El Equipo Mazzanti, a firm devoted to research, design, and the practice of architecture with a focus on the development of projects that build community and thought through lectures and publications. Mazzanti has been a visiting professor at Columbia, Harvard, Princeton, the University of Pennsylvania, the Istituto Universitario di Architettura di Venezia, the Universidad Europea de Madrid, and the Universidad de los Andes and the Pontificia Universidad Javeriana in Bogotá.

Guillermo Hevia García is an architect graduated from the Pontificia Universidad Católica de Chile (UC), where he received the architecture school and academic excellence awards. In 2020 he earned a master's degree in advanced architectural design from Columbia University in New York. He was awarded the William Ware Prize for Excellence in Design and the William Kinne Prize. In 2017 he was awarded the "Young Architect" Prize of the Colegio de Arquitectos de Chile and in 2021 he was included on the Metropolis Future 100 list of top graduating students. Since 2012 he has been a workshop professor at the architecture school of the UC.

Hernán Díaz Alonso studied architecture at the Universidad Nacional de Rosario and earned a master's degree from the Columbia University Graduate School of Architecture, Planning and Preservation. Since 2015 he has been the director of the Southern California Institute of Architecture in Los Angeles.

HLPS Arquitectos is a firm founded in 2009 by Osvaldo Spichiger, Carolina Portugueis, Martin Labbé, and Jonathan Holmes, all architects graduated from the Pontificia Universidad Católica de Chile in 2000. Projects of theirs that have been awarded first place in different competitions include the Parque Cultural Valparaíso, the Teatro Regional de la Serena, and the Rector Eduardo Morales Miranda building in the science department of the Universidad Austral de Chile in Valdivia.

Isaac Broid studied architecture at the Universidad Iberoamericana and earned a master's degree in design at the Oxford Polytechnic (now Oxford Brookes University). In 1991 he was awarded the silver medal at the Bulgaria Biennial and in the 2000 the gold medal at the Bienal de Arquitectura

Mexicana. He has been a member of the Sistema Nacional de Creadores de Arte since 1999 and a member of the Academia Nacional de Arquitectura since 2007.

José Luis Uribe is an architect graduated from the school of architecture of the Universidad de Talca, with a master's degree in the theory and practice of architectural design from the Escola Tècnica Superior d'Arquitectura de Barcelona and a doctorate from the Escuela Técnica Superior de Arquitectura of the Universidad Politécnica de Madrid. He is the author of the book *Talca, cuestión de educación* [Talca: A Matter of Education] (Arquine, 2013), which won the award of the 9th edition of the Bienal Iberoamericana de Arquitectura y Urbanismo and the Deutsche Architekturmuseum Architectural Book Awards (2014). In 2016 Uribe was one of the curators of *A contracorriente* [Against the Tide], the Chilean pavilion at the 15th International Architecture Exhibition of the Venice Biennale.

Josep Maria Montaner is an architect with a doctorate from the Escola Tècnica Superior d'Arquitectura de Barcelona, where he now teaches the theory and history of architecture. From 2004 to 2015 he was co-director (along with Zaida Muxí) of the Laboratorio de la Vivienda Sostenible del siglo XIX. He is the author of some fifty books, including *Del diagrama a las experiencias: hacia una arquitectura de la acción* [From Diagram to Experiences: Towards and Architecture of Action] (2014) and *La modernidad superada. Ensayos sobre arquitectura contemporánea* [Modernity Overcome: Essays on Contemporary Architecture] (2022). In 2005 he received the National Urbanism Prize of the Spanish Ministry of Housing for his newspaper articles. From 2015 to 2019 he was a member of the Barcelona city council and since February 2021 he has been a lifetime member of the Reial Acadèmia Catalana de Belles Arts de Sant Jordi.

JPR Arquitectos is a firm founded in 1972 by José Paul Restrepo Santa María. Restrepo was awarded the Blue Pen architecture prize in Colombia in 2007 and was nominated in 2014 and 2022 for the Mies Crown Hall Americas Prize. His work has appeared in magazines and journals around the world, including *Domus*, *2G*, *Arquitectura Viva*, *Abitare*, and others.

Juan Román is an architect graduated from the Universidad de Valparaíso, with a doctorate in architecture and heritage from the Universidad de Sevilla. In 1998 he arrived at the Universidad de Talca to undertake the project of the school of architecture, of which he was director until 2009.

Mathias Klotz is an architect graduated from the Pontificia Universidad Católica de Chile in 1991. He has worked on residential projects, as well as public and private infrastructure and urban equipment. He has received numerous awards and been both workshop professor and dean of the faculty of art, architecture, and design at the Universidad Diego Portales for the last fifteen years. Several monographs have been devoted to his work and he has received the Holcim, Rogelio Salmona, Borromini, and Aporte Urbano awards.

Mendaro Arquitectos is a firm headed by Ignacio Mendaro Corsini, an architect graduated from the Universidad Politécnica de Madrid in 1974. The work of the firm focuses on the emotional component of architecture. It has earned numerous distinctions, including the Premio García Mercadal in 2004 and first place in the awards of the Fundación PYMECON in 2012.

Miquel Adrià graduated as an architect from the Escola Tècnica Superior d'Arquitectura de Barcelona and has a doctorate in architecture from the Universidad Europea in Madrid. In 1994 he settled in Mexico and since then has been combining the activities of practitioner, teacher, and critic.

He has published more than thirty books about Mexican and Latin American architecture. He is the director of Arquine and of MEXTRÓPOLI | Festival de Arquitectura y Ciudad, as well as director of the school of architecture at CENTRO.

MMBB Arquitetos was founded in 1991 in São Paulo by Fernando Mello Franco, Marta Moreira, and Milton Braga, all graduates of Faculdade de Arquitetura e Urbanismo da Universidade de São Paulo. The firm has received various awards for its work, including that of the Associação Paulista de Críticos de Arte (APCA) in 2015, in the international category, for their automobile museum in Lisbon.

Paula Velasco is an architect graduated from the Pontificia Universidad Católica in 2006, with a master's degree in emergent technologies and design from the Architectural Association in London (2010). She was a finalist of the YAP Constructo program in 2013, with her project of "A Kind of Red Theatre" and was nominated for the Rolex Mentor and Protégé Arts Initiative in 2014. She has taught at the Pontificia Universidad Católica de Chile (since 2012) and at the architecture school of the Universidad Finis Terrae in Santiago. She recently presented her work, alongside Cecilia Puga, at the Harvard Graduate School of Design and the Columbia University Graduate School of Architecture, Planning and Preservation.

Paulo Mendes da Rocha (1928-2021) graduated in 1954 from the architecture school of the Universidade Presbiteriana Mackenzie, where he went on to teach. His works include the gymnasium of the Clube Atlético Paulista (for which he was awarded the prize of the 6th edition of the Bienal de São Paulo), the Museu Brasileiro de Escultura e Ecologia, and the Pinacoteca [Art Gallery] do Estado de São Paulo, which won the Mies van der Rohe Award (European Union Prize for Contemporary Architecture) in 2000. Mendes de Rocha was awarded the Pritzker Prize in 2006.

Plan:B Architects is a design firm established in Medellín, founded in 2000 by Felipe Mesa and Federico Mesa. Felipe is an assistant professor at the school of design and architecture department of the University of Arizona. Federico is assistant professor at the school of architecture of the Universidad Pontificia Bolivariana en Medellín. The two brothers understand architectural design as a provisional pact, a permeable configuration, and a positive expression of the ecological and social conditioning factors that surround us. Their projects and research into the practice and teaching of architecture have been published in four books by Mesaestándar: *Acuerdos parciales* [Partial Accords] (2005), *Esperando la arquitectura* [Waiting for Architecture] (2007), *Permeabilidad* [Permeability] (2013), and *Arquitectura al revés* [Architecture in Reverse] (2017), as well as in *12 Projects in 120 Constraints* (published jointly with AR+D Publishing, 2021).

PRODUCTORA is an architecture firm founded in Mexico City in 2006 and made up of Wonne Ickx, Carlos Bedoya, Víctor Jaime, and Abel Perles. Their work focuses on precise geometries in an endeavor to create legible projects and timeless buildings. The firm has received numerous distinctions, including the Premio Oscar Niemeyer para la Arquitectura Latinoamericana and the Mies Crown Hall Americas Prize for emerging architecture.

Wonne Ickx studied civil engineering and architecture at Ghent University in Belgium and urban studies at the Centro de Estudios Metropolitanos (CEMET) in Guadalajara, Mexico. He has taught architecture at Harvard, Princeton, Columbia, the Illinois Institute of Technology in Chicago, the University of California at Los Angeles, and Rice University in Houston, as well as at several universities in Mexico. He is a cofounder of LIGA, Space for Architecture, an independent platform in Mexico City that has promoted contemporary Latin American architecture since 2011.

Rogelio Salmona (1927-2007) studied architecture at the Universidad Nacional de Colombia in Bogotá. In 1948 he traveled to France, where he worked in Le Corbusier's atelier. In 1958 he returned to Bogotá, becoming involved in the world of academia and beginning his own architectural practice, devoted to single-family residences, multi-family housing developments, and large urban works. He has received numerous distinctions both at home and abroad, including the grade of officer of the French Ordre des Arts et des Lettres (2007), honorary membership in the American Institute of Architects (2006), the decoration of the Great Order of the Colombian Ministry of Culture (2006), the Manuel Tolsá Medal of the Universidad Nacional Autónoma de México (2004), the Alvar Aalto Medal awarded in Finland (2003), a doctorate *honoris causa* from the Universidad Nacional de Colombia (2000), the Prince Claus Award (1998), and recognition at several editions of the Bienal de Arquitectura de Colombia.

Salvador Macías Corona is an architect who graduated with honors from the Instituto Tecnológico y de Estudios Superiores de Occidente (ITESO) and went on to earn a master's degree in the theory and practice of design from the Escola Tècnica Superior d'Arquitectura de Barcelona. He is a member of the Guadalajara chapter of the Academia Nacional de Arquitectura, a design professor at the ITESO (since 2003), and a founding member of the Estudio Macías Peredo. He is also a member of the Fundación de Arquitectura Tapatía Luis Barragán and the founder and director of the architecture space Jardín 17, part of the Casa Luis Barragán in Mexico City. He has received two silver medals from the Academia de Arquitectura de Jalisco and several honorable mentions for his architectural work, as well as the Premio Obras CEMEX in 2020.

Smiljan Radic is an architect graduated from the Pontificia Universidad Católica de Chile, with further studies at the Istituto Universitario di Architettura di Venezia. In 1995 he founded the firm Smiljan Radic Arquitecto. In 2001 he was named the "Best Chilean Architect" under the age of thirty-five by the Colegio de Arquitectos de Chile and in 2009 he became an honorary member of the American Institute of Architects. His work includes the design of the pavilion of the Serpentine Gallery in 2104 and the "House for the Right-Angled Poem" in 2012.

Sol Camacho studied architecture at the Universidad Iberoamericana and the École Nationale Supérieure d'Architecture Paris Val de Seine, before going on to earn a master's degree in architecture and urbanism from the Harvard Graduate School of Design. From 2004 to 2006 she worked at Architecture-Studio in Paris and at SOM and TEN Arquitectos in New York. From 2012 to 2014 she was a partner of METRO Arquitetos in São Paulo, where she undertook projects with Paulo Mendes da Rocha, and worked with OMA in the same city. In 2014 she founded RADDAR, an architecture firm devoted to research and design in São Paulo. Camacho curated the Brazilian pavilion at the Venice Biennale in 2018 and exhibitions between 2017 and 2020 at the Instituto Bardi, founded by Lina Bo Bardi and located in the Casa de Vidro in São Paulo.

Solano Benítez graduated from the architecture school of the Universidad de Buenos Aires in 1986 and has spent his career as a member of different collectives. His work has received the "Work of the Decade 1989-1999" award of the Colegio de Arquitectos de Paraguay and the second edition of the Contemporary Architecture Prize of the European Union for Latin America in 1999. Benítez received an honorable mention at the Congreso Nacional Paraguayo in 2011 and since 2012 has been an honorary member of the American Institute of Architects. He has represented Paraguay in architecture biennials in São Paulo and Lisbon. He won the Golden Lion as best individual participant at the 15th edition of the Venice Biennale in 2016 and the Global Award for Sustainable Architecture in 2021. He cofounded Gabinete de Arquitectura in 1987.

TAAU (Taller Abierto de Arquitectura y Urbanismo) was created in 2004. It has since consolidated its position as an architecture and urbanism firm focused on design, graphic communication, and the comprehensive development of projects on different scales. It has undertaken housing projects, public and cultural buildings, urban design, infrastructure, and public space, as well as joint projects with acclaimed Mexican and international architects, such as the Museo Jumex in Mexico City, in collaboration with David Chipperfield Architects, for which it was awarded two first places in the Premios Obras CEMEX.

TALLER | Mauricio Rocha + Gabriela Carrillo was founded in 1991 by Mauricio Rocha, an architect graduated from the architecture school of the Universidad Nacional Autónoma de México (UNAM), a member of the Academia de Artes, and a lifetime member of the jury of the Marcelo Zambrano architecture scholarship. Gabriela Carrillo, also a graduate of the UNAM, was a partner between 2012 and 2020. TALLER received the Emerging Voices award of The Architectural League of New York in 2014. The architects have lectured in various cities in North and South America, Europe, and the Orient. Their work has been presented in exhibitions and architecture biennials, as well as in books and magazines in Mexico and abroad. Some of the their designs are in the collection of the Centre Pompidou in Paris. In 2019 TALLER was awarded the gold medal of the Académie d'architecture in France.

Taller de Arquitectura X. Alberto Kalach is a laboratory, a greenhouse, and a research team in Mexico City that has created a place to explore, question, and redefine the notion of space. They have endeavored to transcend the inevitable geographic, economic, and temporal limitations of a given project and transform them into an opportunity to build solutions that not only respect and celebrate the environment, but also serve the cultural context by allowing it to see itself being built. Their concern with the emerging problems of the big city is often reflected in their work: from the minimal five-thousand-dollar home to larger housing developments, and even the biggest project ever conceived in the Valley of Mexico, called *México Ciudad Futura*.

Tatiana Bilbao ESTUDIO was founded in 2004 in Mexico City. The firm focuses on the analysis of the context surrounding its projects, from masterplans to typologies of affordable housing. In 2019 the firm's work was highlighted in a series of Architect's Studio exhibitions organized by the Louisiana Museum of Modern Art. It has also presented its work at the Graham Foundation, the Chicago Architecture Biennial, the Venice Biennale, the Museo de Arte Contemporáneo de Monterrey, the Museo Amparo, the 'T' Space gallery in Rheinbeck, New York, and the Centre Pompidou in Paris.

Tatiana Bilbao was a consultant for the Department of Housing and Development of the Mexico City municipal government. She has been visiting professor at the Yale School of Architecture, the Harvard Graduate School of Design, the University of California at Berkeley, the Architectural Association in London, the Columbia University Graduate School of Architecture, Planning and Preservation, Rice University in Houston, the Universidad Andrés Bello in Santiago de Chile, and the Peter Behrens School of Arts in Düsseldorf. Recent distinctions include the Tau Sigma Delta Gold Medal of the Association of Collegiate

Schools of Architecture (2020) and enrollment as an honorary fellow of the Royal Architectural Institute of Canada (2021). In 2022 she received the Richard Neutra Award for Professional Excellence.

Teodoro González de León (1929-2016) studied architecture at the Escuela Nacional de Arquitectura. He worked in Le Corbusier's atelier in 1947-1948. His works include El Colegio de México (1976) and the Museo Rufino Tamayo (1981), both in collaboration with Abraham Zabludovsky, the Mexican embassy in Berlin (2000), with Francisco Serrano, and the Museo Universitario de Arte Contemporáneo (2008). He received the Premio Nacional de Ciencias y Artes in 1982 and the Medalla Bellas Artes of the Instituto Nacional de Bellas Artes in 2012.

Teresa Moller is an acclaimed Chilean landscape architect who has been working in the field for thirty-five years. She taught herself over the years, working on a variety of projects of different scales, including Punta Pite, the Parque Periurbano de Calama in Chile, and works in Shanghai (China), Cumelén (Argentina), Sydney (Australia), and Corsica (France), as well as a permanent exhibition for the Internationale Gartenausstellung in Berlin (2017). She was invited in 2017 to participate in the Venice Biennale and in 2018 to be a juror at the Barcelona Architecture Biennial. In 2020 she was nominated for the Global Award for Sustainable Architecture sponsored by UNESCO for her contribution to sustainable development.

Víctor Alcérreca Molina is an architect who teaches workshops at the Universidad Iberoamericana and at CENTRO. He has collaborated as visiting professor in programs for Mexico City at the University of Arkansas and the University of Washington. He writes about architecture and the city.

Zaida Muxí Martínez is an architect and professor of urban planning at the Escola Tècnica Superior d'Arquitectura de Barcelona and is on the faculty of the association Arquitectes de Cabecera. A specialist in urbanism, architecture, and gender, she is a member and cofounder (in 2015) of the network "One Day, One Architect." She was the director of urban planning, housing, environment, urban ecology, public space, public circulation, and civic responsibility in Santa Coloma de Gramenet from 2015 to 2019. Her recent publications include *Beyond the Threshold. Women, Houses and Cities* (dpr-barcelona, 2021), and *Política y arquitectura. Por un urbanismo de lo común y ecofeminista* [Politics and Architecture: For an Ordinary, Eco-Feminist Urbanism], co-authored with Josep Maria Montaner (Editorial GG, 2020).

+UdeB Arquitectos | Felipe Uribe de Bedout is a firm founded in 1990. Uribe is an architect and urban planner graduated from the Universidad Pontificia Bolivariana in Medellín. He has taught at the undergraduate and post-graduate levels and has lectured at numerous international universities and institutions. His public works have contributed to the urban renovation and social rehabilitation of Medellín, earning distinctions at home and abroad, such the honorable mention of the Premio Latinoamericano de Arquitectura Rogelio Salmona (2014), second international mention at the 19th edition of the Bienal Panamericana de Arquitectura de Quito (2014), the Internazionale Marmi e Macchine Carrara award (2001), in the external facing category, the Premio Nacional de Arquitectura Martínez Sanabria at the 17th edition of the Bienal Colombiana de Arquitectura y Urbanismo (2000), and the Accésit de Arquitectura award of the 2nd Bienal Iberoamericana Arquitectura e Ingeniería Civil (2000).

Photo credits

Germán Valenzuela: p. 20
Blanca Zuñiga: p. 21 (top)
Juan Román: p. 21 (bottom)
Héctor Labarca Rocco: p. 22 (top)
Daniel Priet Labbé p. 22 (bottom)
Ximena Céspedes: p. 23 (top)
Luis Calquin: p. 23 (bottom)
Javier Rodríguez: p. 24 (top)
Felipe Aranda: pp. 24 (bottom), 25 (bottom)
Mauricio Ureta Villagra: p. 25 (top)
José Luis Uribe: p. 26
Ximena Cáceres: p. 27
Jonnattan Silva: p. 28 (top)
Carolina Solís: p. 28 (bottom)
Edgard Torres: p. 29
Angélica Méndez: p. 30
Katherine Carrillo: p. 31 (top)
Antonia Ossa: p. 31 (bottom)
Pia Montero: pp. 32, 33
María Jesús Molina: p. 34
Hangysan Sahueza: p. 35
Courtesy of Felipe Uribe de Bedout. Alejandro Arango: pp. 42-49
Cristhian Sainea: pp. 56-58, 64, 65
Brenda Soto: pp. 60-61
Gabriel Ossa: pp. 59, 63
Rogelio Salmona: p. 62
Roland Halbe: pp. 72-75
Jorge Gamboa: pp. 76, 78 (bottom), 79
Alberto Fonseca: pp. 77, 78 (top)
Tadeuz Jalocha: pp. 86, 87
Xavier Ribas: pp. 88-91
Guy Wenborne: pp. 98-99, 100 (bottom), 101, 188-193
Teresa Moller: pp. 100 (top), 102 (bottom), 103
Estudio TMSA: p. 102 (top)
Courtesy of AGENdA: pp. 110-111
Jaime Navarro: pp. 124-127, 354-361
Margot Kalach: pp. 128, 129
Yoshi Koitani: pp. 130-133
Bertolino Barrado Arquitectos: pp. 140-147
Pedro Hiriart: pp. 154-161
Leonardo Finotti: pp. 170-179, 216-223
Iwan Baan: pp. 186-187, 258-263, 292, 296-297
JAG Studio: pp. 200-201, 202 (bottom), 204 (bottom), 205, 206, 207, 209
Francisco Suárez: pp. 202 (top), 203
Andrea Vargas: pp. 204 (top), 208
Cristóbal Palma: pp. 112-117, 230-237, 304-313, 368-379, 386-393
Rafael Gamo: pp. 244-251
Luis Gordoa: pp. 270-271, 273, 276 (top), 278
Sandra Pereznieto: pp. 272, 274, 275, 276 (bottom), 277, 279
Courtesy of Museo Jumex. Fernando Marroquín: pp. 286-291, 293-295
Courtesy of Ignacio Mendaro Corsini. Fausto Nahum Pérez: pp. 320-325
Courtesy of MMBB Arquitetos. Sergio Souza: pp. 340-341; Ana Mello: pp. 342, 343, 345, 347; Nelson Kon: pp. 342 (bottom), 344, 346, 347 (bottom)

25 Works & 25 Voices was printed and bound in August 2022 by Artes Gráficas Panorama in Mexico City. It was set in typefaces of the Graphik family and printed on 120 g Bond paper. The print run was 1,200 copies.